# CHANGING SCENES

**John Mercer**

# CHANGING SCENES

by

**John Mercer**

NEW MILLENNIUM
292 Kennington Road, London SE11 4LD

Copyright © 1998 John Mercer

All rights reserved. No part of this publication may be reproduced in any form, except for the purposes of review, without prior written permission from the copyright owner.

British Library Cataloguing in Publication Data.
A catalogue record for this book is available from the British Library.

Printed by Morgan Technical Books Ltd.
Wotton-under-Edge, Gloucestershire
Issued by New Millennium*
ISBN 1 85845 210 4
*An imprint of The Professional Authors' & Publishers' Association

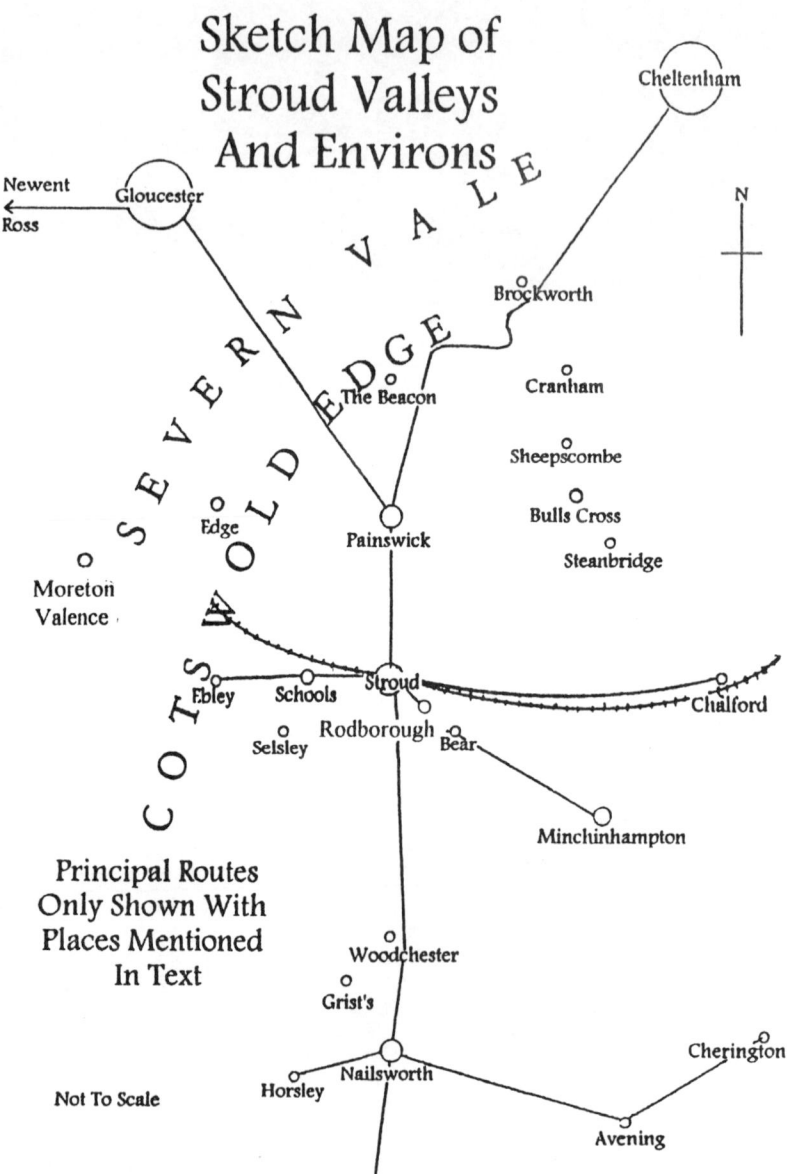

# CHAPTER 1

The village church was filled with soberly clad figures, no concession here to the summer sunshine so far as dress was concerned, in 1939 Sunday was still the day when one wore Sunday Best, weather notwithstanding. With parents and younger brother I had been brought from our holiday hotel arrayed in the new uniform of the junior school which I was to start attending in a few weeks time, grey flannel shorts and braided jacket. At rather less than nine years old I could just about see to my front in the church as I stood wedged between my father and mother.

At some time around the middle of the service I saw a man walk up the church and hand a piece of paper to the vicar. Having read the message he announced that war had been declared.

Strange that I still have a clear recollection of that man and his piece of paper when so little of that summer holiday readily springs to mind. A child from a very protected environment, I could have no idea of what that announcement meant in definition, let alone in practical consequence. Yet I was surrounded by all those churchgoing adults for whom there had been scarcely twenty years of peace to fade the memories of parents and brothers slaughtered in the First World War. Now the worst had happened, after all the years of hoping that war could be avoided, with all the months of local defence planning, Britain was once again at war. How much did they know about this second war? No doubt the biggest single obvious difference from last time was going to be aerial attack, but beyond that would we win or lose, conquer for right or be enslaved by evil, survive or die?

My young mind had no preconceived images or memories

to torment it, but that announcement helped to justify my father's decision to spend our summer holiday in Gloucestershire rather than go to France as in the two previous summers. I certainly was not prepared for the extraordinary change of course my life would take within the next two weeks.

In my beginning was Home, a house on the outskirts of London near Wimbledon, where I arrived a couple of weeks before Christmas 1930, after something of a tussle as I learned years later, under the expert supervision of a Queen Charlotte's nurse; of course. Sixteen months later when my brother arrived a Queen Charlotte's nurse again attended, of course. I could not appreciate it then, but the greatest stabilising influence in my early years was the fact that there was a right way of doing things. What other people did was of no consequence, nor did we have any contact with them to disturb our nice secure certainty.

Gradually we developed through crawl and totter to explore this house where we lived. It was double-fronted, the hall running right through from the front door to the kitchen across the back, with the scullery beyond. Right of the hall lay the dining room leading back to father's study, whilst to the left two rooms had been made into one long drawing room with two fireplaces, a bay window to the front and a glazed door at the back into father's conservatory, a wonderful place with its own heating system where grew tall orchids and fragrant carnations.

Upstairs at centre front the bathroom looked over the garden as did our parents' room to the left, with the children's room behind overlooking the back garden. Uncle David had the right hand front room, and at the back over the kitchen was the maid's room.

Let me introduce the small population of our tiny world. First of course mother, ever present, ever patient, ever loving, only later to be seen ever correcting, restraining, protecting. Then there was the maid, a strange figure in a way because in fact she was plural, since maids essentially came and went over time. Moreover she had in each case a sort of dual identity. In the mornings she helped mother with the housework and lunch preparation wearing a blue or green overall; then she disappeared and emerged at four resplendent in black dress and starched white apron and headdress to produce and serve afternoon tea.

Father was a somewhat shadowy figure at first, we were confined to our room until he had gone in the morning, and it was usually only after our six o'clock bathtime that we would be brought down to say goodnight as he sat in his armchair. At week-ends father had his hobbies in the garden and conservatory, his stamp collection and the work he brought home and he must not be disturbed.

Last but far from least uncle David, who came to be so important to us in those early years, and doubtless to our parents as well. Like father he was gone before we emerged in the morning, re-appearing about bedtime, but he was at home on Saturday and Sunday afternoons and occasionally on Sunday mornings as well.

Indoor play confined us to the big warm kitchen with its coke range where the flat irons stood, with the lovely Landseer monochrome print of a stable interior on the wall. A green baize covered door sought to keep the noise of domestic activity from the rest of the house. In time, when we were steadier on our legs, the back yard became available for play, still under mother's eye as she watched us through the big kitchen window. It boasted a small shed where the perambulator lived with some of the larger toys.

That pram was a splendid conveyance. Coachbuilt high prams were still fairly common but they did have a certain prestige value. When we were parked outside a shop I now realise that the pram was positioned in front of the window not simply to enable mother to keep an eye on us. A half mile round trip showed us the sights and enabled mother to do the shopping. Fresh food had to be bought regularly, for though we had a nice cool larder there was no refrigerator. The milkman with his horse-drawn float delivered, as did the baker with his little van. The Sunlight laundry had a big white van, but the coal merchant still used horse power.

The quiet tree-lined road with its bay windowed brick houses closely grouped behind their little front gardens on each side ended where the railway line to Waterloo cut across on a big embankment. Here we turned left passing a row of shops where most of mother's purchases were made. Pleasantly uncrowded at our time of day it was a scene of housewives passing along the pavement while delivery drivers nipped back and forth from van to shop. Occasionally there were added joys for the young pram passenger. The sound of the barrel organ was always exciting, audible a long way ahead. At the entrance of a little side street we would find it, the organ-grinder standing beside the two little shafts by which he pulled this strange instrument along, turning the handle that somehow produced odd jerky music, while his little monkey with its collar and chain held the bowl for contributions.

Some of the delivery vehicles were magnificent, but by far the most impressive was the great covered waggon which brought Atora suet to the shops, drawn by two enormous long horned oxen. So often it was sheer size that stuck in the memory, like the great cart horse teams pulling the brewery drays, with their beautifully polished and decorated harness and their nose bags slung beneath the dray with the wheel wedges and skids.

Grocer, butcher, baker, greengrocer and fishmonger were all in this little line of shops, and then came the turning back up the gentle slope towards home, a street parallel to our outward route of small solid detached residences with little front gardens. With the shopping safely stowed beneath the pram floor we made our stately way to the short stretch of road linking the two streets I have mentioned, where stood our home.

Unseen at first, for it stood well back, its location could be spotted from a distance by its twin front gates, one at each end of the frontage, both leading by the same curved pathway to the front door, that path and the front fence bounding a semicircular bed of standard roses. Our return took us to the further gate and another path down the side of the house to the back door.

Gradually of course we grew and became more mobile and perceptive. Our range extended from the back yard down the narrow path beside the smelly old coal shed to the back garden. The main lawn had a big pear tree in the middle, a small vegetable patch with another pear behind rambler roses beyond, and towards the house father's hydrangea and rhododendron beds. Against the far fence an old open summer-house contained tools and chairs. Exploration was always under mother's watchful eye, to trip on the cinder dressed path could result in a nasty graze. Grazes were one thing to be avoided at all costs as they warranted the agony of tincture of iodine. Once stung by that yellow staining horror never forgotten.

The pram stayed in its shed, and we graduated to walking that shopping circuit. Half way to the main group of stores we found Mr. Trimmer's little sweetshop where we could sometimes be bought a tiny conical bag of dolly mixtures weighed out from one of the many glass jars ranged on the shelves. My own favourite were miniature butter drops, the size of peas but without the menace afforded by full size boiled sweets if you had the misfortune to swallow one. Ahead we could see the green electric trains passing on the embankment, while on the road past the shops below the quiet red double deck trolley buses with their long backward sloping antennae followed the overhead cable lines.

That little row of shops always had their awnings and side panel blinds fully extended, they faced almost due south as I now realise. The draper did not want her displayed fabrics to fade and the others must keep their wares cool. The butcher's meat display, the grocer with his big slab of butter and stacks of bacon rashers, and the fishmonger had great marble slabs in their windows on which to arrange their wares. There was so much sawdust on the butcher's floor that you could slide, there of course to mop up blood, and the white tiled walls echoed to the thud of chopper on block. Mince for the children, a couple of kidneys, sweetbreads, tripe or liver for father's supper, and the week-end joint; were all ordered for delivery as needed.

The grocer had other attractions for us. A long low rack in front of the counter held glass topped biscuit tins containing all manner of delights to crave while mother ordered the bacon. Unhooked from the rack in the window the side would be grabbed by the great spikes of the big red Berkel slicer. The assistant quickly turned the handle on the great flywheel, the bed ran back and forth across the cutter, the rashers falling neatly onto the sheet of greaseproof in the assistant's left hand. Number seven on the Berkel scale gave mother's required thickness. I never saw unsmoked bacon, only real dry-smoked.

In our nice secure way brand loyalty flourished. Untempted by advertising mother stuck to Cooper's Oxford marmalade, jams by Wilkin of Tiptree, cheese biscuits were Jacobs's high baked water, sweet biscuits always by Huntley & Palmer, whether ginger nuts, rich tea or Osborne. Lux flakes washed our small clothes, the laundry took the rest. Persil never had a chance, I seem to recall that its advertising was felt too plebeian. Nor would Bisto gravy browning ever be found in our home, it used quite the wrong advertising image with those two children called 'Bisto Kids'. Children were children, kids either small goats or young Americans; with neither category had we any contact.

Beneath his blinds the greengrocer's colourful display extended onto the pavement; then last in the line, and the shop where we always wanted to look, the fishmonger. The centrepiece of his sloping marble slab was often some rare or odd creature trawled up from the deep, menacing of appearance, now fortunately harmless. Here too would come the ice cart, dripping under its tarpaulin, whence great slabs of ice were slid to the pavement and dragged into the shop by the ice man in his hessian apron using great pronged tongs.

Fortunately we had two different small parks nearby where less restricted but still very much accompanied play was possible. In the near corner of Melbury gardens were see-saws and swings, Holland gardens provided a sunny expanse of mown grass surrounded on three sides by tall trees and on the fourth by a line of red hard tennis courts. Both were about three hundred yards from home. Sometimes mother took us there.

But mention of play introduces uncle David, so often the one to take us out to play or keep an eye on us. Unlike tall lean father he was no more than middle height, somewhat rotund, and a generation older than our parents. Of course as children we just accepted him as one of the family, it was only long afterwards that one began to realise the key role he played beyond supervising our play. A bachelor, he had lived in Ealing before father and mother married, and was a friend of both their families who also lived there. Neither parent was well off and uncle David became an invaluable paying guest and family friend. As a young man he had worked in British Guyana and South Africa before returning to qualify as an analytical chemist.

Now he was public analyst for the borough of Bermondsey and took the train to Waterloo each day and the bus to his laboratory. On Saturday afternoons he could be relied upon to take us out, and again on Sunday afternoons. On Sunday morning he often took the train to town again to attend church either at Westminster Abbey or St. Paul's depending on who was preaching.

Unlike mother, whose 'No's and 'Don'ts' became positively nerve-wracking when she was looking after us, dear uncle let us explore and extend our experience; and as we grew older he too often got scolded when we came home in muddy clothes. Up on the hill beyond the public gardens lay Wimbledon common, a place to run without danger, to watch kite flying, model boats on the ponds, and play a wonderful form of hide-and seek which involved crawling among the birches beneath the canopy of the tall summer bracken. Here too in autumn were colourful fungi, poisonous and to be strictly avoided we were told.

Most professional people worked five and a half days a week in those days, and father left home to catch his train at 8am, seldom returning before 6pm. He would have had precious little time with his wife had there not been uncle David to take charge of the children for a few hours at the week-end.

My picture of father at that time is mostly of a tall lean man in city suit and bowler striding down the garden path to catch the morning train, (did mother really let fall a sigh of relief as the gate clicked shut behind him?) or alternatively of a furious figure wringing his hands and biting his lip; about to embark on one of his explosions. I do not remember any physical violence but his sheer ferocity terrified the lot of us.

He was, as I learned long years later, an only child brought up largely by his mother; his father having disappeared from the scene when the boy was quite young. Only very moderately off, his mother managed to have him articled to a firm of city accountants, where in due course he qualified as a Chartered Accountant, and enjoyed travelling to conduct audits in the West Country.

When in his early thirties his mother died, leaving him free to marry my mother. By now he was secretary of St. James's club in Piccadilly, the principal club for the diplomatic community. His was fascinating but demanding work as I now realise supervising one of the finest dining facilities in London while in constant correspondence with important personages from all over the world. Years later his envelope collection contained the handwriting of such people as Axel Munthe and Von Ribbentrop. Sadly in our early years the principal emotion he stirred in us was fear. One had to eat properly, speak properly, and have one's hair brushed properly. His own dark hair showed a precise left side parting and single tight natural wave, and he despaired of our fluffy child hair. I can feel his two ferocious hairbrushes now. Even when we were out in the pram mother always had her little camel hair brush in her bag and constantly corrected the damage caused by the breeze to our appearance.

Father never enjoyed robust health though all the time I knew him he was a great worker, and when we were quite small he had a bad attack of pneumonia. Combining convalescence and a business trip he sailed to New York and back, by Cunard of course. We were too young to notice his absence.

Our days were filled with mother, as we played with our various push-along toys on the kitchen floor, or our pull-along toys in the back yard. She made our meals and taught us to eat them, making minimal fuss when we chose to dislike something. In the early days she had made and knitted some of our clothes. Wool was the great thing for children, and those awful itchy tight things I had to wear are with me now. Each night she bathed us and sat beside us as we said our prayers before turning off the light. She seldom had time to read us a story at that stage of the day. But she certainly encouraged us to read, and well before going to school we had made good headway with our Blackie readers. Copybooks too were provided, ruled and with example letters to be copied many times over to produce a copperplate hand. Early learning of a most useful kind, but still in a tiny bubble of life devoid of contact with other children, a situation that still continued after we had started at school, since we had no contact with the other children after school hours.

The great social event of our week, and absolutely terrifying to this very shy little lad, was Sunday Lunch. After enjoying our meals in the familiar warmth of the kitchen during the week, we now had to be spruced up to join the adults at the big table in the dining room. When younger brother arrived to oust me from the high chair I graduated to a hassock placed on a dining chair, where I had to sit bolt upright without benefit of chairback. Mother's place at one end of the table kept her in easy reach of us two children, one on each side of the table. Father sat at the opposite table end behind the sirloin. When all was ready he rose and said grace, then taking the carvers he would say to mother

"Shall I serve the children first?"

"Yes please dear" was the reply.

The sirloin was turned over, the fillet cut out and a couple of tiny slices put on our two plates to be passed down to mother. Having done such cutting up as was needed she added potato, squashing it well into plenty of gravy, Yorkshire pudding, then vegetables, but very carefully as we disliked most of them and would squirm and otherwise show dissent if given more than a tiny amount.

"May they begin?"

Thank you for letting
me know about
your op.
Hai, hoping all
goes well. Let
me know.

love G.

Mr K Vale
24 Bournham Mead
Rodborough
Common
Stroud
Glos GL5 5DZ

"Yes" replied father, still carving for the grown-ups.

Uncle David was usually there, and sometimes another aunt and uncle, or perhaps grandma and grandad. We were slow eaters and seldom had to wait long for pudding while the adults finished their beef. Once again we would be served first, and liking most puddings would finish well ahead of the parents. Now for the great embarrassment of the week. We actually had to speak, in front of all these adults, all looking at us and smiling encouragingly as we gabbled our lines. It went like this.

"Shall I let the children go?" asked mother.

"Yes, please dear"

"What do you say?"

"Thank-you-God-for-my-nice-dinner-amen-please-may-I-get-down-excuse-me-Mummy." We bolted from the room.

Sheer torture, the sweat pours down my neck sixty years later, but now we could go and play quietly while the grown-ups carried on the conversation they might have had but for the 'not in front of the children' convention. This would have ruled out all topics of adult interest until after our departure.

Mention of grandma and grandad introduces two people I very clearly recall. Mother's mother was a tiny wizened little person, unflattered by thirties clothes, skinny enough to look frail to my young eyes. Grandad, though not as tall as father, had a very erect, almost military bearing, his grey moustache neatly waxed at the ends, grey trilby worn well forward. Blazer and neatly pressed grey flannels, polka-dot bow tie and meticulously polished shoes complete my picture. They lived on a tiny smallholding in Essex, coming to stay with us at Christmas, and sometimes in the summer. Our visit to them must have been our first trip away from home.

We travelled by local electric train to Waterloo, taxi to Liverpool Street, and then to Billericay, this time in a train with a corridor, and a real engine at the front. Vast London stations with great puffs of smoke and steam billowing up into their lofty roofs, filled with strange sights and sounds of every kind astounded us.

It was all a tremendous adventure, that great hive of activity at the rail termini where porters pulled luggage trucks while trains, vans and taxis came and went, passengers were always hurrying, and each great train noise was promptly followed by its echo from the roof far above. Then looking out at all that countryside rushing past, providing our first view of cows and sheep the train puffed and rattled along, bumping over the rail joints and rocking so much that you had to hold on tightly when standing.

We were met at the station by uncle Harold with his car, yet another first for that day, we had never travelled in a private car. Small wonder that my unfortunate brother revealed a weakness for travel sickness.

The yard outside grandad's front door contained a big kennel housing two large black Labradors, each chained to an iron ball. To the right, backing onto fields were a number of chicken runs bounded by high wire mesh. To the left a vegetable patch was being broken in, the hard yellow clay lay in lumps where it had been turned up, now grandad was hacking it into submission with a spade. We took a turn at the job, banging away with hoes, but it was a hot day and we were soon tired. Recollection fails at this point; no doubt at the end of such an exciting day I slept most of the way home.

We would meet the grandparents again when they came to stay for Christmas. Preparations for that feast started months before. Christmas to me is always brown. One day mother would assemble a vast range of ingredients, far too much to handle in her largest mixing bowl. The great brown glazed bread bin, its wooden lid removed, became the centre of pudding making activity. Brown raisins were slit and de-seeded with great care by mother, then there was brown sugar, brown stout, brown brandy; after these and all the other ingredients had been mixed you could look into that bowl and everything was brown. There followed a very important ceremony when each of us was lifted in turn to stand on the kitchen chair beside that great brown crock, and armed with a monster wooden spoon try to stir the mixture. As you did so you were able to make a wish. This last needed thought well in advance, and you must keep it to yourself. Of course it invariably concerned Christmas presents.

Now the great oval tin steamer with its fitted thermometer was brought out and cleaned for its annual task, and bowl after bowl of pudding mix was filled and tied down under cloths for cooking. Next came the mincemeat making, another brown mixture filling the kitchen with strange smells and a range of one and two pound jam jars of spicy pie-filling.

Next mother would go to her bureau and take out her card index, ready to write a large number of Christmas cards. I have never felt happy about this operation, you had to do it because if you did not you would receive no cards to clutter your mantelpiece and other furniture. But two index checks were needed, one to note your card sent, and after Christmas to record from whom you had received a card; only then could they be discarded when the children had tired of playing with them.

As the great day approached we were kept occupied with packs of coloured paper strips and a gum pot as we joined together the ends of each strip through the previous ring to form paper chains. Decanters appeared on the sideboard, but most of the decorating happened after we had gone to bed.

The day itself arrived as if by magic. We had been put to bed with dire warnings against waking and frightening Father Christmas away, a pillow slip hung from the end of each of our beds in the hope that a stocking would not be big enough. Then in the morning came the happy scramble through all the wrappings to find a great range of presents while mother struggled to list what had come from whom, ready for the thank-you letter task.

Downstairs meanwhile the grown-ups had wrought a wonderful transformation. From the top of the stairs the hall could be seen festooned with paper chains, holly along the picture rail, and a big bunch of mistletoe hanging inside the front door. Next came the unforgettable smell of the Christmas tree. A peep into the double drawing room revealed two bright fires, side tables set with sugared almonds and other sweetmeats, and the special multi-drawer box of chocolates that father always brought home from Fullers for mother at Christmas. Mantel shelves were decked out with Christmas cards of great variety. Everywhere gay paper chains radiated from paper bells and balls fixed to the ceiling.

And there in the front bay window stood the tree, in its great tub, not far short of ceiling height. It was draped with tinsel and hung with coloured glass balls and foil-wrapped chocolate shapes, little bundles of tablets, and gold mesh bags of foil covered imitation coins. Every evening until Christmas was over we would each be able to choose one of those chocolate decorations before going up to bed. Then too there were the candles, real spiral shaped wax candles about four or five inches long, stuck in punched tin sconces with clips beneath to hold them to a branch. Each day father would light them for a time, and pinching them all out was a rather smelly business.

The dining room too was draped with paper-chains, holly sprays topped the frames of the ancestral oil paintings, and nut bowls, biscuit barrel and baskets of fruit had joined the decanters on the sideboard. The dining table, now fully extended, had colourful and rather terrifying crackers at each place. This was no time for us to play in the busy kitchen, uncle David took us for a walk while lunch was made ready, and we enjoyed looking at Christmas trees in other front windows.

And so to the feast, signalled by a firm roll of the gong, then a frightening volley of crackers, after which the rubbish had to be collected, paper hats put on, and other odd cracker contents became the topics of chat while father carved the great brown turkey. Christmas must always be special for the things that only appear at that time, but of all the turkey, stuffing, pudding and the like my abiding favourite remains bread sauce. When all at table had enjoyed an ample sufficiency the bird was removed, the curtains closed, and the pudding was brought in. Father poured brandy over it and a match produced a display of dancing blue flames. Mother continued basting with the flaming spirit until the blaze subsided. It was an enchanting sight to young eyes, but the flavour of Christmas pudding seemed too spicy for me.

Then all to the drawing room, and comfortable armchairs while the children played beneath the grand piano. Here, beyond the carpet edge, our toy cars ran free on the polished floorboards without disturbing the adults. Gradually the other great aroma of Christmas filled the room, the men were drawing gently on their Havana cigars. A cigar lasted about three quarters of an hour, by which time the room had grown very quiet as one by one the ladies, and then their menfolk had nodded off, and we both crept quietly out to continue our play upstairs in the bedroom.

Unfamiliar and over-rich food naturally resulted in degrees of digestive disorder, but so far as we children were concerned mother's medical arsenal showed little variety. While we were still at the inarticulate howling tummy-pain stage Woodward's Gripe Water was the remedy. I retain a very soft spot for this potion, a clear sweet watery liquid which I always remember as the only medicine I ever took which actually tasted nice. I could have enjoyed a double dose at any time. My reaction was fairly natural, it has been pointed out recently that you could get quite nicely high on the stuff if you took sufficient.

Milk of Magnesia I did not like, though there was not a lot of flavour about it, but Petrolagar was worse, a slimy business like a mixture of paraffin and face cream. Worst by far in flavour, and reserved for the solidly costive, was syrup of figs. Prescription medicines for our coughs and colds were all quite horrible. Preventive tonic on the other hand, to build us up for the winter provided a compensating treat. Cod liver oil and malt came as a spoonful of thick treacly toffee we both really enjoyed.

I do not think we troubled the doctor very often, but there was one purpose for which the entire practice descended on our home, or so it seemed to me. Three and a half was the age at which children's tonsils were removed. Recollection is of course a bit fuzzy but I do remember waking up and being given ice-cream; several times in fact, and that was a unique event. The next year I had a better picture of the scene as younger brother's turn arrived. Uncle David had vacated his large double bedroom to stay at his club in London for the night. In the morning there was much activity and I was told to keep out of the way. Doctor Rose was our doctor, but the brass plate listed Bradley, Lessey, Rose, Metcalf and Smith. Add a nurse and it seemed as if the whole lot were going to appear. In a lull after the initial activity I crept into uncle's room to find the big bed pushed aside, and in its place an austere operating table with overhead lights and anaesthetic kit with nasty rubber mask. On a nearby table, ranged on a white cloth were a hideous array of shiny instruments and those awful solid rubber gags on chains the dentists used. Small brother was confined to his bed so I naturally gave him a detailed account of the scene. I was firmly told that that was not a very kind thing to do; meanwhile he went on howling.

Soon my world was to expand into years of dreary routine at school, but first we would enjoy our first really long-distance journey, to holiday at St. Ives in Cornwall. Our local station at Raynes Park was approached by a steep slope, Wimbledon however, next up the line towards Waterloo had its station below street level, an easier approach for trolleys of heavy luggage. So we set out for Wimbledon by hire car, open hire car at that to minimise any problems of car sickness. The cabin trunk and cases were strapped on the outside baggage rack at the back, the last suitcase on the front wing opposite the spare wheel. Fortunately the weather was dry. There we joined the electric train to Waterloo where once again we met the awesome din of a big rail terminus. Motor horns, train and guards whistles, lorry engines roaring and fierce steam discharges echoed back off the high roof.

Father had reserved a compartment on the express, some dozen coaches linked by a corridor, with restaurant car near the middle. St. Ives passengers travelled in the rearward coaches. With the freedom of movement afforded by a whole compartment between mother, father, uncle David and ourselves we could hardly have been more comfortable, but that journey lasted many hours, and as the train neared its destination we children were very tired.

The train stopped. We hardly noticed after all those stops we had made earlier. But in fact this was very different, because after a little while the train started moving once more, but in the direction whence it had come. And now someone played a little joke on us children. "There you are, now we are going home again". We cried our eyes out, scarcely noticing our first ever view of the sea as the train made its final approach almost along the beach to St. Ives.

For that station had been St. Erth, where the main front part of the train continued to Penzance while the rear St. Ives coaches were uncoupled and taken by another engine the few remaining miles to St. Ives. Over the years I have developed a deep affection for Cornwall, but the name of St. Erth commands something else in my memory. Soon we were taxied to a local boarding house up a little distance from the beaches, fed, watered and bedded down.

Next day we began to experience the sights and sounds of the seaside, the wheeling gulls, the boats, fishermen, harbour and of course the lovely beach with its wonderful sea, never silent and never still. Rocks and tide pools provided new discoveries everywhere, and the sea air left us very ready for bed when the time came to go back up the hill to our boarding house.

Two very special memories remain with me from that holiday. The first was a commonplace event. We were walking down a steep little street towards the harbour, the upper floors of the houses on each side projecting beyond the ground floor towards the building opposite. Down the middle of the cobbled street ran a gutter. With a warning shout of "gardy loo" somebody pitched a bowl of slops out of an upper window into the gutter. The total lack of response from people walking in the street confirmed that this was a very ordinary sight. But it just happens to be the only time I have seen the practice of dumping slops in this way, and I have never heard that warning call since.

The other abiding recollection is one of great excitement. In the boathouse facing the broad harbourside roadway stood the great lifeboat on its launching trolley, its broad blue snout towering haughtily above the passer-by, and even higher above us children. One day as we walked near the harbour we heard a loud explosion high above, it was the launching maroon. Suddenly the town crier appeared in his red coat, white stockings and tricorn hat calling everyone to haul on the launching lines. Everybody, natives and holiday makers, young and old, started running to the harbour.

The slip was not opposite the boathouse, rather the trolley had to turn west along the harbourside to a slip just outside the inner harbour. By the time all the crew were aboard a great crowd were ready, ourselves among them, with our hands on the heavy ropes that would haul the lifeboat to the slip.

With all that available labour the trolley was soon manoeuvred to the top of its launching slip, then with a great rumble of bogie wheels and an enormous splash the lifeboat was away and heading to seaward. Sixty years on I still treasure than memory too, because on our next visit to St. Ives two years later the crowd of launchers had been replaced by a tractor.

We slid down the great sand dunes at Sennen, dug the beach at Porthmeor to make our first, rudimentary, bucket sized sandcastles, and collected shells from the little rock pools. I was too young to realise that by Christmas of that year, 1934 I would have passed my fourth birthday, that schooldays would soon follow and that sixty years would then elapse before I could once again find freedom from routine in one form or another.

A painful lesson was learned on that holiday, our young shoulders quickly became covered in big yellow blisters, calamine lotion eased the pain but the cause was clear, ours was the sort of skin that had to be kept covered up.

The fact of course was quite the reverse, it was because our clothing offered no exposure that we had had no chance to become hardened to a little sun and sea air. Close-fitting wool knits over woollen underwear were our constant itchy lot. The blister problem would be solved by a later holiday next year, at a more northern location, September in the Isle of Man.

# CHAPTER 2

And so at last I started at school. A private preparatory school about half a mile away towards Wimbledon had been chosen, the quickest approach being a zig-zag route through quiet residential streets for most of the way before we joined the main road with its trolley buses and commercial traffic, and the parallel railway line close beyond. To school and back was therefore a walk, but on the first day it was also a most important revelation. We were hardly out of our own front door before I saw for the first time The Great Black Tide.

From all the streets further up the hill streamed hurrying figures, converging into a great mass at the top of Lambton Road for the final rush to Raynes Park Station. Black shoes, dark suits, black bowlers or homburgs, black brollies, this all male army strode grimly on looking neither to left nor right, exchanging no word with anybody as they went. Not one happy face was to be seen. I had never seen the morning rush hour before but that morning provided more education than I had gained in all my few very protected years. Of course I knew there was something called money, mother handed it to shopkeepers when she bought things, but whence it came had not previously occurred to me. It was just one of those matters that we were not to be worried about at our age. But father joined that grim army every morning, and now it gradually dawned on me that he went to Town to do something for which somebody gave him money, certainly not because he just liked to go there. It was the great lesson of my kindergarten days, and I learned it before I had even reached school.

Our route turned left from the Townward throng along a bright little street edged with laburnums, then right on another of larger houses set well back from the great plane trees lining the pavement. Another left, another right and then straight along to a corner house where three ladies presided over our little group of boys about to start their years of formal education. It was a bright, warm and comfortable place, and I was not too hopelessly shy because I had been introduced to the school and staff a few days earlier. The small scale of things here also helped to make me feel less exposed, nursery size furniture and desks matched mine at home.

Writing copy books and Blackie readers too were in the same series I had started, but there were new activities as well. Protected by aprons we tried our messy hands at modelling clay, much more fun than my Plasticine, you could actually make things to keep because the teachers would bake our efforts after school and by the following day they would be hard enough to take home. My models were not very ambitious but did produce a bit of fun. Forming a small cup shape from the wet clay, I would then press the lip in one place against my little finger. Turn it over and you had a tiny igloo. On our clover covered back lawn each bloom had its bee, and my game was to drop the igloo over a bee and watch it crawl back out of the igloo door. My younger brother was unlucky, he was stung, very loudly indeed.

The daily walk to and from school took the lid off Pandora's box, as awareness gradually dawned that there was real life beyond our little cocoon. We still listened to Ann Driver's music and movement on the wireless in the morning, only now we moved in a group at school, and we still listened to uncle Mac and Toytown after tea. But in our little travels we saw lots of men doing different jobs, dustmen, bus drivers, postmen, gardeners, shopkeepers, roadsweepers, firemen and so forth, and we came to realise that all grown-up men did jobs. From this stemmed the idea of choice, and having decided that I wanted to be a bus driver I later graduated following our next main line journey to a preference for becoming a train driver.

We could see too that small boys became bigger boys going to bigger schools, for when we peeped through the knot holes in our playground fence we could see on the junior school playground next door boys who had been in our little class the previous year. Our experiences were now expanding rapidly, far faster than our knowledge, and they were therefore still disjointed, a jumble of jigsaw pieces in a bag, only a fraction of the number needed to form a real picture.

There was that Isle of Man holiday, our first steamer trip where me met an uncle and aunt of great antiquity living in a remote and very overgrown cottage. We were taken to London Zoo, a fantastic place where people crowded round to see the new baby chimpanzee with its mother, a whole lot of firsts for us here meeting all those strange and foreign creatures. Kew gardens too was a fascinating outing, most especially the great tropical house with its tall palms and the water-lily with leaves so vast a small child could sit on one.

Shopping trips became more extensive, even as far as London on occasion when a visit was needed to the essential schoolboys' outfitter Daniel Neal. Unlike our leisurely local streets London was all rush and din; buses, barrows, taxis, carts jostled noisily in the roadway while pedestrians hurried everywhere. Klaxons, cart bells, roaring engines and the shouts of hawkers and news-vendors made pavement conversation almost impossible. Here is another example of an incomplete picture, what I then called London extended little further than Oxford Street, Regent Street and Piccadilly.

But there came a day when even Piccadilly stood still. Late in January 1936 King George V died, and the state funeral route included that street. Father's office at St. James' club had a balcony overlooking the route and Green Park beyond, and he managed to arrange for us to watch the procession from that magnificent viewpoint. After an early start we emerged from Green Park underground station to find troops already lining both sides of the road, quiet black coated crowds already gathering. Well wrapped against the winter chill in our tweed overcoats with their black crepe armbands we hurried across the road to the warmth of the club.

Soon church bells all over the town began slowly tolling and from the distance came the sound of muffled drums. We took our places on the balcony to find the great crowds now gathered below looking away to our right for the first sign of the procession. Having then just passed my fifth birthday I must be careful not to let imagination take over from memory. There came a seemingly endless succession of service units and bands, the latter all with muffled drums, and playing sad music, and then at last the lines of naval ratings holding the long white ropes by which they hauled the gun-carriage bearing the coffin. Then came heavily cloaked men on horseback, followed by horse drawn carriages, and finally more service units and bands.

All that long time in the cold on the balcony had left us in urgent need to relieve our bladders, and we were taken to the somewhat palatial club urinal. Now we had come across the plate glass anti-splash angled at a height to protect one's shoes before, but here the arrangement was different, that glass was positioned above knee high to an adult. We quickly solved the problem, and standing well back used the impressive muzzle velocity peculiar to small boys to launch our stream in an arcing upward trajectory, howitzer fashion, over the rim of the anti-splash. St. James' was the principal club of the diplomatic community, so many of whom would have crowded into London that day to represent their various countries in paying respect to the late king. Numbers of them too must have had good cause later in the day to welcome that excellent facility which we two youngsters had treated so irreverently. Of course we did not spot the humour in the situation at the time.

Our horizons were expanding, but our social contacts were still very tightly controlled. I did have a birthday party where ten selected small boys came to tea. I did not enjoy it, partly because I was still very shy even with my classmates, and more so because I did not like to see other children playing with and sometimes damaging my new toys before I had had a chance to try them myself. We came from widely different backgrounds, and I remember once going to a friend's party at a big house by Wimbledon common where he had a ride-on railway in the back garden. His nursery also contained a magnificent rocking horse, something we could never have found space for at home. The fact is that I was not good at making friends, and circumstances did not offer much encouragement.

Then, at last we had an opportunity to learn that life did not always have to be a matter of glum obedience. We went to visit mother's sister who lived with husband and two children near Billericay in Essex. Cara was a little older than her brother Roger, my brother and I rather younger still. Our cousins lived in a house with a long garden. The swing was in constant demand, but far more important, at the bottom of the garden was a dense hazel thicket and a wood. Unfortunate elder cousin was constantly burdened with the warning "You're responsible" when we were all let out to play. But that was the end of her responsibility because Roger, with his mischievous smile, would shout "come on" and leaving Cara the three of us would dash off to the wood. We had a wonderful time in a totally adult-free environment building dens and hunting each other with nobody to restrain us. This was a completely new definition of enjoyment, provided by the additional ingredient of freedom.

We had no inkling that in a mere three years we would have nothing but the countryside in which to find our amusement.

Still more experiences were added to our collection. We visited Hampton Court Palace, the British Museum, and Croydon aerodrome. This last was a memorable day, Croydon being the principal airport for London at that time, not many miles from our school, and we were always on the look-out for the great new passenger aircraft of the day. We must have visited on some sort of show day because I remember walking around among huge parked aircraft, all sitting on their little tail wheels and tall undercarriages, nose in air.

Unfortunately we were not taken to London for the coronation of King George VI; presumably it was felt that the crowds on that occasion would be far more boisterous than on the day of the funeral procession we had watched from the club, and we ought not to exposed to that sort of thing. But compensation was soon to follow; after another holiday at St. Ives father had despaired of the English summer, this year we would go to Brittany for a month.

I had moved on from the snug little kindergarten with its three blue overalled lady teachers to the preparatory and junior school next door, and found the whole thing thoroughly daunting. So used to speaking only when spoken to I could not cope with adult staff looking like real teachers, and other pupils of whom I was still hopelessly shy. But I could keep up with the learning, and I have to admit there was one great aid to integration used at that school which I have not seen elsewhere.

At the end of the playground the blank brick wall of the gym had a cricket wicket painted on it. About ten feet on either side of this a white line painted down the wall extended across the playground for some twenty yards. A bowling position was similarly paint marked. No fielder could stand within the two long lines. A tennis ball was bowled and a crowd of lads waited along the fielding limits to retrieve it, others preferring to stand deep toward the far end of the playground. A batsman could be out either bowled or caught, in which case the bowler took the bat. If the batsman played a successful stroke the next ball was bowled by the fielder who had retrieved it. It was in fact a very fast game, morning break did not last long and everybody hoped to win his turn to bat. Here the whole school competed keenly in what was very much a game of chance, and breathed a lot of good fresh air in the doing. Most of us were blowing a bit as we ran back up the steps when the bell sounded for the next lesson.

Summer 1937 came and we were off to Brittany, all six of us for grandma and grandad came too. An evening train from Waterloo to Southampton was far less tiring than a rail trip to Cornwall, and then we boarded the St. Malo ferry where we were comfortably tucked up in our bunks. Despite the strange surroundings, the noise and the motion we were not sick, and there in the morning was the dockside, the long customs sheds and the enormous train. The nearer we approached the higher the train towered above, each carriage even had steps for passengers to climb in. At last the answer dawned on me, French railway platforms were not built up to carriage door level as in England.

Geography lessons had shown that there were other lands beyond our shores, and those not marked in red on the map spoke different languages from our own. We had been introduced to very elementary French, but we still needed to be protected from having to use it. After all, the words were odd enough, but odder still was the way the native French spoke them. Fortunately we had two communicators in our party, mother who spoke good French, and father who was always very clearly understood. I have always admired his technique, much used by the British abroad for centuries I suppose. He just spoke clearly, slowly and just a little loudly in English.

As the train pulled away from St. Malo the countryside looked much like our own, but after a couple of hours the sun became brighter and the land flatter and drier. At last the train was running slowly beside pine woods, and the next stop was La Baule, our destination. La Baule really is sand and pine woods, the famous three mile south facing sweep of sand beach backed by the hotels and town built on sand, where shade giving pines flourish, their aroma permeating every part and building. Shining wood floors kept carefully polished added to the effect, pine polish was used daily after the sand brought in on feet had been swept.

Our suite at the Grand Hotel was nicely compact in one corner of the first floor. Father and mother had the corner double bedroom, grandma and grandad another double on the side of the hotel, my brother and I next to our parents on the front of the building. Each room had its own private bathroom with lavatory, washbasin, bath and another fitting I had not seen before.

Rather like a lavatory, it had no flush box or water trap; instead there were hot and cold taps. Mother explained that it was a foot bath for washing off the sand. Of course, with all that sand everywhere you went, I really ought to have been able to work that out myself.

Standing on our balcony in the heat of that first afternoon the sea was mirror calm fading in the distance to a hazy mirage. The gentle ripples breaking on the beach were hardly audible. To right and left, just the width of the road away, was fine sand as far as the eye could see. Fortunately our skin had hardened somewhat with time and cool windy holidays in England, and now beneath an almost cloudless sky we were going to sample a little lads' holiday heaven. Soon we were off across the road in our woollen one-piece swimsuits, with our buckets and spades, then into that quiet cool friendly water, quite unlike the boisterous sea we had known until now.

It was a simple routine, daylight woke us before breakfast arrived, and we would creep out of bed onto our balcony in our pyjamas to watch the sea and the early traffic. There came a sharp knock on the bedroom door, we sprinted back to our beds, pulled up the sheets and chirped "Ontray". The door opened and in came the smiling maid, putting our breakfast tray on the table. "Bonjour messieurs" she said, to which we replied "Bonjour mademoiselle" as she departed. That last word really was a bit of a tongue-twister.

Mother came in to pour our tea, and we set about the novelty of eating hot croissants, rather dangerous because inside was either very hot jam or very hot chocolate. The best I can say for these continental breakfasts is that they gave us a good appetite for lunch. Then off to the beach with the big holdall of clothing changes to be put in our square beach tent. Long lines of these stretched along the top of the beach; and when not in use for changing the front was lifted to form a square awning where the grown-ups could sit in their deck chairs in the shade. We had now graduated to building rather more elaborate sandcastles, though we never entered any of the frequent competitions. Donkey rides, bathing and ball games occupied us, with walks along the beach to admire the equipment of the various gymnastic clubs and see what all the other holiday makers were doing. All too soon it was time to cover up from the fierce sunshine, and we returned to the hotel for lunch.

First a quick wash and brush up, then down to the big dining room with its wide sunblinds. So different from bland home meals, our keen appetites left no time to consider whether we would or would not like the unfamiliar dishes on the menu. The hors d'oeuvres trolley was a great attraction, not only because it was the first offering to appear, but for the fascinating variety of colourful dishes it displayed. We joyfully tucked in without much regard for the fact that this was only the starter, Main courses, cheeses, desserts and fruit followed. There were of course diversions. Once grandad selected a really beautiful pear, yellow with a reddish blush I remember, and neatly ran his dessert knife round it. As the two halves fell apart on his plate a large red grub marched indignantly out to our muffled amusement. Father turned in the direction of the head waiter, raised one forefinger and two eyebrows and suddenly plate, pear and inhabitant were gone, replacement pear and profuse apologies instantly provided.

After lunch one retired to bed for an hour or more, it really was too hot for the beach, then later we would walk into the town in the shade of the pines to explore the scene, always including in our circuit Renou, the ice-cream shop. Small round marble topped tables on black cast iron pedestals stood beneath big fans mounted on the ceiling above, the shop window filled with magnificent gateaux, pastries of many kinds, and the parents' favourite, rum babas. Renou provided the only vanilla ice-cream I have ever eaten where dark specks of real vanilla pods could be seen in the dish, its flavour was incomparable.

But there came a day when we nearly missed our trip to Renou. It had been an exceptionally hot morning, and perhaps we had had just a little too much sun, for when we retired to our room after lunch both of us quickly became very uncomfortable. Acute tummy ache was followed by really spectacular scarlet diarrhoea. Mother was very worried, the hotel manager summoned the doctor. By the time he arrived we were flat on our backs in bed, having been told to keep still and keep quiet. The doctor asked sensible questions about what we had been eating, we meanwhile were loudly protesting that there was nothing the matter with us, for the thought of French medicine filled us with horror. It emerged of course that the hors d'oeuvres had been our downfall. Lovely oily sardines, with olives, celeriac and a delicious dish of diced beetroot garnished with chopped fresh herbs and garlic all liberally doused with olive oil had provided a formidable emetic. The doctor proclaimed us fit just in time for our trip to the patisserie.

It was here at La Baule that I first began to develop my interest in fish and fishing. The fishmonger's slab at home, fascinating as it always was, could not compare with the fish markets here. Tuna hung like bombs from rails above, sacks of shellfish fronted the display, where huge crawfish many times the size of a lobster shared the slab with smaller crayfish, crabs, octopus, and fresh sardines together with other fish more familiar to our experience.

At the eastward extremity of the bay stood the little harbour of Pornichet, and on the seaward side of the harbour wall were mounted jibs from which square nets hung from four ropes, rather like an inverted umbrella. These nets could be lowered or raised by a little hand winch. Their existence was justified by the fact that food fish sometimes passed close inshore, a point we once saw illustrated on our own stretch of beach. Some local fishermen had been watching a shoal from the shore. As it came close in a rowing boat quietly paid out a net in a long semi-circle, finally passing the end to others on the beach. Very quietly, in order not to frighten the fish which might otherwise dive under the net, fishermen and holidaymakers slowly hauled it in, finally landing a sparkling heap of sardines.

Having had nothing more than a bit of crumbed plaice fillet for Friday lunch at home, I was delighted to find how deliciously tasty these little fish are. Whether hot or cold they often featured on the menu and encouraged us to try other fish dishes. A walk to the fishing boat harbour of Le Pouliguen at the other end of the bay, and the bus trip to Le Croisic a few miles further enabled us to see real fishermen with their boats, nets and pots, not unlike those we had seen at St. Ives. But the catches they were landing were very different, all those wonderful creatures we had seen on the market, many of which came to our dinner table. For the most part these dishes were served very attractively, but on one memorable occasion the presentation was, to our English eyes, impossible. A plate of cooked crayfish in their shells was placed in front of each of us, covered in a hot thick sauce. Obviously one was expected to eat them with the fingers, equally obviously one was going to get in a filthy mess. Father really came into his own, as one responsible for one of the best tables in London he required extra napkins, and finger bowls. Only he made much more of the opportunity than I have, and seemed to continue snorting and seething for some hours afterwards, having made his justifiable annoyance obvious to all those in the dining room.

It was a wonderful holiday, and we returned to school aware of a bigger world where small boys existed in much greater variety than our little school group, and speaking many languages. Gaining daily in knowledge we felt we were living in a very exciting time. There were so many new advances to talk about, the first regular flight to Cape Town followed only a couple of years later by the first scheduled flight to Australia; and the great race to build ever bigger and faster passenger liners. On land Sir Malcolm Campbell, George Eyston and John Cobb were competing for the world speed record, and all of their strange looking vehicles were represented in my little garage of Triang model cars.

School continued as before, but we were acutely aware of the developments in civil aircraft as one great new machine after another flew in to Croydon almost over the school. We visited the Natural History Museum with its immense prehistoric animals, and the Science Museum where all kinds of strange devices were demonstrated, far beyond my comprehension; and we saw our very first film, Snow White and the Seven Dwarfs. Very pretty, but I did not much enjoy sitting in that hot dark cinema for such a long time.

All through the winter, and the spring of 1938, the one thing we both wanted to do was to go back to La Baule. We were very fortunate, father had booked the same rooms for our summer holiday We left grandma and grandad to look after our home and took uncle David with us instead, and he proved very useful. Over the past year there had been more and more talk of war, and now, on the beach at La Baule it became our favourite game.

Early each morning children hurried across to the beach while the sand was still wet from the night tide and started digging trenches in a zig-zag line towards the sea. The English and French dug one line, while the Germans and others dug another about ten yards or so away. Ammunition was provided by squeezing wet sand, snowball fashion, and stacking the product on shelves cut in the front wall of the trench. There followed a great game of grenade throwing at the opposite side, until the stocks of sand balls were exhausted. Then uncle David, fluent in German and French, walked down between the trenches to arrange a cease-fire; whereupon both sides rushed down to the sea to fill buckets of water for the manufacture of more ammunition.

That firm wet sand behind a falling tide was also ideal for cycling, and on hired bicycles we began to learn how to pedal fast enough not to fall off. Soon we could ride faster than uncle could follow, and we pedalled away along the beach past the really big hotels like the Royale and Hermitage and the casino. When we realised that we could no longer recognise our own hotel among the endless line of buildings fading into the distance we became very slightly scared and turned back. Bicycles of our own were still many years away, but we had acquired a basic skill of great importance without experiencing the nasty reality of falling off on a rough hard surface.

It was another holiday in brilliant sunshine, but this time we were led to feel that next year we would have to go somewhere different; rather a pity, but we accepted the idea, parents knew best and there were some matters where one instinctively knew that it was best not to ask why.

School went on as usual, but the routine now included regular practice at putting on and wearing our gas masks, ugly uncomfortable things that we had to carry around in their little cardboard box hanging from a strap over the shoulder. Christmas came and went, and it was decided that next September we would change to another school. Interviews and discussions followed, uniforms were bought, and one very shy little eight year old did not look forward at all to having to meet a whole new crowd of boys all far bigger and more numerous than before, and a lot of really daunting looking masters who rushed around trailing black gowns. Such had been my memory of that interview visit.

We were still too young to understand much about the international situation, but we were sometimes still playing when father switched on the wireless to listen to the news. He had bought an HMV autoradiogram, a great chest which contained both a radio and a record turntable capable of playing six twelve inch records one after the other. It certainly added to our available amusement because he had included in his record collection a number of items for children. Loudspeakers in the kitchen and dining room could relay wireless or records.

That Christmas we not only had uncle David playing his piano to entertain the family, but father's popular classical and London show records as well. As we played under the piano with the clockwork Hornby train set that uncle had given us our world seemed much the same as it had been a year earlier.

But there was still no question of a summer holiday in France. The decision had been taken and we would go with mother and father to Gloucestershire to visit great-uncle Willie and auntie Lou. Willie was the last member of mother's family still living in the area where large numbers of her relations had dwelt in earlier generations. Once again the great hire car was piled with luggage, but this time we were off to Paddington, where the cream-striped brown carriages of the Great Western railway, huge steaming green engines at their front, hauled famous services including our Cheltenham Flyer. We had been in a train before, but this journey was different. Time after time it seemed we dashed straight through quite big stations, then at last stopping at a little country place called Kemble.

For some time now the engine had been working hard, though the green countryside with its pale farm buildings seemed fairly level in the bright sunshine, but things were about to change. All along the train windows were being closed, we were about to go into a long tunnel. For a minute or two the train pulled busily away, then suddenly the lights came dimly on and we were in the tunnel. One more short length of sunlight and it then became really dark with the grey engine smoke racing back along the train. The engine seemed more relaxed now, yet we were gradually going faster. That tunnel went on for a jolly long time.

Then suddenly to our right we were looking down into a steep green valley, the train running down along its flank until as it neared the valley floor the sprinkling of cottages gave way to massed terraces. The dramatic scene change from the gentle world above the tunnel to this most beautiful hillside picture beyond will always remain an indelible memory. Now the little stream and derelict canal beneath us as we left the tunnel had been joined by a road, and together with our railway line followed the valley bottom. Soon the train stopped again at Stroud, and we got out, our baggage being portered to a taxi. How strange, I thought, that after all those nice pale stone houses we had seen on our approach, and this nice matching railway station, we should now find a great red-brick factory filling our view to the hillside.

Our taxi managed to drive us right up that long steep hill until we had a wonderful view of hills and valleys in all directions, and there, right on the top, was our hotel, the Bear. A swinging bar guarded the archway entrance to the inner courtyard, where stood a great stuffed bear. In the last century travelling entertainers had often been accompanied by some animal to draw the crowds, this bear had been a performer's attraction. The hotel was very comfortable and had magnificent views, but there was no sand beach, and no sea. This was not going to be much of a holiday as I saw it. Instead the hotel was surrounded on three sides by fresh cow manure, another novel experience for our noses and our shoes.

We had driven up past the steep banks of Rodborough Common, and beyond the constricting walls of the Bear and the properties opposite the common opened out again in a broad and more extensive expanse toward Minchinhampton. Cattle were turned out to graze these commons, and ponds in various locations encouraged them to move around over the available pasturage. One such pond lay very near the Bear, and the large trees overhanging the road by the hotel gave welcome shade from the mid-day sun. The animals congregated there and deposited their thank-offering before moving on. Our noses preferred the seaside air, but we quickly learned to tread warily.

It was not a very happy time, and this different holiday underlined the harsh changes which threatened, and of which we were now at last becoming aware. A few weeks earlier a news tragedy had occupied us for the very first time. With other radio listeners everywhere we had waited for days until it became obvious that apart from just four survivors the seventy crew in the submarine *Thetis* had died in their ship on trials in Liverpool bay. There was talk too of moving children from the east coastal towns to areas less liable to attack; was there going to be a war or not, and what did war mean? We really had no idea.

Bus trips to local towns provided our amusement for the most part, afternoon tea with scones and jam and assorted pretty little cakes meant it was time to catch the next bus back to the hotel. Of course we did visit uncle Willie in his lovely double fronted bay windowed cottage facing south over the valley at Chalford, and auntie Lou's scones were particularly nice. In the wood behind the cottage were badger holes, and by listening carefully with your ear close to the hole you could hear them snoring; provided your hearing or your imagination were good enough. The dry stone wall bounding the path through the little orchard to the summer-house hid lizards which loved the hot sundrenched stones and soon emerged if you kept quiet.

We nearly took up golf. Quite close to our hotel Minchinhampton common had a golf course, though we saw more cows than golfers. Father had played golf in earlier years, and now in Woolworths we found nice little putters just the right size for small boys, with a neat cast iron head set to a wooden shaft. Soon we were learning to putt on the common. It is of course a precise skill, and does not offer the explosive expenditure of energy that a young under-exercised lad needs to express. We had to learn to hit that ball really hard if we were going to get some satisfaction out of golf. Our little putters assumed the role of drivers, and the balls went all over the place.

A bit of instruction was needed. Father stood behind,

reaching down and holding the wrists of the boy with the club, then taking him slowly though the correct sequence of club and body movements designed to send the ball in the desired direction. The idea was good but it took no account of our need to get on with our play, as we saw it. Patience was not our strong point. Father was coaching my brother when up came an explosive backswing, wrists very slack, and the iron club head struck father just above his right ear with a horrid thud. Standing behind him and able to follow the full sequence of events I must admit I behaved quite disgracefully. Father grabbed his head and started running round, head down, in ever decreasing circles. For some reason this strange scene tickled me and I found myself laughing uncontrollably. Brian, initially facing the wrong way to see where his club head had struck, turned round to see me laughing and father staggering round while mother rushed to grab him and steer him tenderly back down the road to the hotel. Father was as white as a sheet, there was no blood, and I remember wondering whether he had any. It could have been much more serious, but in the event a couple of days in bed brought a full recovery.

There came that Sunday when we went to Minchinhampton church, and the vicar announced that war had been declared, and that memory keeps company with two others only so far as that holiday was concerned; our first observation of cows and more specifically of the need to avoid the back end of them, and my brother's failed attempt at accidental patricide.

The next morning father went to Stroud on his own, and came back to tell us that he had obtained a house at Painswick. We boys would not be returning to London, mother would live with us at Painswick while he returned to his work at the club. We simply could not comprehend the implications of that decision, changes of school, home, surroundings, recreation, would dawn upon us gradually as they arose, but one thing was certain. As we had gone through that train tunnel from the level farmlands to the steep wold edge we had passed from one world to another. The future held nothing but doubt at every level. Our cosy ordered assured way of life might not survive. This then was the end of my beginning.

# CHAPTER 3

Our new home could hardly have been more different from the double fronted house at Raynes Park, which stood well back off a quiet residential road. Now we were shown a narrow slice out of a line of adjoining houses fronting directly onto the main road, right in the middle of the village. Unlike its neighbours it thrust its bay windows out well beyond the general line of buildings, narrowing the pavement. Obviously we were going to see and hear a lot more now of whatever village life would be in future.

From the front door a stone flagged passage ran past the living room, stairs and dining room to the back door, which opened onto a yard. Immediately outside was a shallow sink and pump, drawing from the well in the cellar. To the right ran a high wall, and to the left lay the kitchen extension, followed by the fuel store. From the far end of the yard stone steps led up to the long garden, with flower borders followed by lawn and then a vegetable plot which boasted a big apple tree. The whole garden sloped toward the house, with the result that occasionally in a big thunderstorm the water would flow down the garden path, in at the back door and out at the front to the street, but that was something for us to learn later. A coke stove provided hot water, but all the main rooms, bedrooms included, had fireplaces.

Furniture quickly arrived, some from our London home, more from second-hand shops in Gloucester, a new gas cooker and carpets. Curtains were less important because the war regulations imposed a black-out; it was an offence to show any light outside at night and windows had to be fitted with shutters to that end. Soon we had a habitable home.

Meanwhile our future schooling had been arranged. To the west side of Stroud four secondary schools were situated close together, first two single sex central schools, then the girls grammar school and farthest the boys grammar school, Marling. At that time there was a preparatory class at Marling school, and in order to assist such as ourselves who had moved by reason of the war the entry age was lowered by one year, and I just qualified for admission. My brother on the other hand went to the girls High School at first, which had a pre-preparatory class for boys. All children travelling from a distance to any of these schools used the school buses. For those of us around Painswick the Western National provided a big green double decker which stopped directly opposite our house. Entry was via a low platform with grab rails at the back of the bus, then up one step to the lower deck, or up the curving stair to the top deck. The girls all used the lower deck, boys taking their more riotous behaviour up the stairs. Prefects made sure that reasonable standards prevailed.

On our first day mother led us across the road and put us in the charge of a senior High School girl, and hoped for the best I suppose. I certainly had no intention of sitting downstairs with a lot of girls, and soon joined the noisy company upstairs. Communication was a terrible problem. In all that jumble of voices I could hardly recognise a word, I had never come across regional English accents before and kept my mouth shut for the most part. Once at school the speech of staff and pupils was more intelligible, nearer to the south London pseudo-Oxonian I had been taught, but after school the other youngsters on the bus greeted any speech of mine with puzzlement and ridicule. There was only one thing to do, learn their language and as quickly as possible. In a week mother was saying that she could not understand a word we said. However badly, we were both speaking in a broad Gloucestershire accent. With time of course mother too learned the native accent, though she never used it.

The buildings of Marling school presented a heavy grey dumbbell appearance, the substantial headmaster's house linked to the lofty hall with its surrounding classrooms by a covered cloister walk. Handsome wrought iron railings over a stone retaining wall bounded the frontage and continued past the school entrance along the edge of the playing fields. Further back behind the hall the school had extended, one corridor passing the gym and continuing with classrooms on both sides to physics laboratories at the far end. Another shorter corridor branched right beyond the gym with more classrooms. In the angle of these buildings stood the woodwork shop, including more importantly the tuck shop, and beyond that the chemistry laboratory. It was a neat and colourful picture, the grey of the original school set off against the brick of the gym, workshop and laboratory, while the classroom corridor buildings were clad in dark creosoted timber on brick bases.

    The far boundary of the school grounds was formed by the main Great Western railway line to Gloucester and Cheltenham. To the westward the whole depth of the site was laid to cricket pitches, with a modern pavilion centred at the top against the railway fence. Winter rugby games were played on another field on the opposite side of the approach to the school.

    War, however, had come to spoil the scene, contractors were digging zig-zag trenches along the far side of the cricket field, with numbered entrances at intervals. Within were wooden benches, and occasional recesses with hessian curtains contained bucket latrines. Roofed in with corrugated iron sheets covered in excavated soil the smell of damp bare earth pervaded the interior. On hearing the wailing siren of an air raid warning classes were to proceed in orderly fashion under the supervision of their teacher to their allotted entrance. Crossing that wide playing field took time, and I remember a number of practices, when many lines of boys could be seen walking quickly toward their entry, but we would have been a marvellous target for a machine gunner. I do not recall using the trenches during an actual air raid alert.

It was some weeks before the new preparatory form intake became aware of the full extent of the school. Our class room was one of those in the original building, where a number of rooms opened from the two sides of the main assembly hall. Of all places our room was next door to the headmaster's study, the staffroom next beyond ours. It seemed a pretty daunting spot where one had to behave absolutely correctly at all times; I felt thoroughly intimidated. Fortunately the school bus reached its destination in ample time for us to get to school and take off our navy gaberdine raincoats before the bell started to ring for prayers. We had no reason to be among those coming on foot or bicycle who had to start hurrying at the start of that bell to avoid having their names taken for being late.

The singing master took his seat at the piano front right, we all filed in with Songs of Praise words editions, juniors at the front and older boys further back, even filling the steeply tiered gallery beyond the back of the hall. Gowned masters lined the sides, the bellringer stopped and the headmaster entered front left from his office. He read notices, we all sang a hymn, then came a reading, another hymn and the grace. The choir led the singing but we hardly needed them as the hymns were so easily singable in those days. Good beefy stuff for the most part, and a bit of patriotism was not out of place in the uncertain days at the start of the war; when many of our number had waved goodbye to brothers or fathers off to the front, and others knew that they would soon follow. Many singing at the start of that new school year would themselves be called to the colours before hostilities ceased.

Prayers over we filed the few steps to our classroom,

where we remained unconscious of the outside world until mid-morning break. It was a lofty room, and the windows, though amply large, were too high for we small folk to see outside. Soon those windows were criss-crossed with adhesive paper tape as a precaution against flying glass from bomb blasts.

A large proportion of the class were local boys, new to the school like the rest of us, but a year older than me. The remainder had come there by reason of the war, and an odd bunch we were. Some were foreign, of what nationality I had no idea, some were only now going to learn English, but I dare not ask their story in case they had left parents or brothers behind, whether living or dead, in some Hitler occupied land. In any case my shyness still protected me from enquiring. Diligently and with varying success we applied ourselves to our learning.

The handbell ringing for morning break revealed another world. From the cosy blinkered cocoon of our classroom we emerged onto the playing field perimeter drive to find a vast clamorous throng. The biggest boys could only be distinguished from teachers by the absence of a gown, then there were the slightly smaller ones walking and chatting in groups. Next came a noisier type whose conversation was louder and less relaxed, punctuated by horseplay in one form or another, and gradually one became aware of those only a year or two our senior, though obviously at home among this great crowd. My hope was that I would grow to be as comfortable in my surroundings as these.

As it happened our routine had no opportunity to become established. Thousands of folk from the midlands had already arrived in Stroud under government evacuation arrangements, and now we found that we must share our school with Handsworth grammar school from Birmingham. This would be achieved by starting the school day earlier, working mornings only six days a week, with games in the afternoons, during which Handsworth had the use of the buildings. The three other Stroud secondary schools were not affected, with the result that though all still travelled to school together, Marling boys returning home before the normal end of afternoon school had to catch an ordinary service bus, most of which started from Stroud. I soon had plenty of practice running the better part of a mile to catch a bus, then often standing panting for forty minutes waiting for the next one.

Although some bus services ran only every two hours, three served Painswick at different times which reduced the travel problem. My term-time season ticket cost one pound nine shillings and threepence and was valid on any bus on any day of the week. There were no Sunday services. Soon our green Western National fleet was joined by some evacuated Oldham Corporation buses in chocolate and cream livery, our Red and White coaches by Midland Red.

I was far too young to appreciate the organisation involved in all these changes, and I could not claim to be disturbed by them, after all I had had no chance to settle to a routine since leaving my London home. Suddenly the nights were drawing in and the need for lights in the evening made completion of the black-out shutters urgent; we did not want to invite a German bomber nor the local policeman.

Soon too mother would need fire-lighting wood, and we had to start our never-ending job of gathering fallen twigs to help with the daily task of keeping the house warm. This was our introduction to the nearer local woods, the springboard from which we graduated to more distant exploration in the coming years.

We just had time to get some idea of the layout of the village before the dark evenings arrived. Opposite our home the big churchyard with its tall railings and yew trees filled the view, the great spire of the church rivalling any we had seen in our part of London. The long line of pale stone houses to our right was broken by a pub, with a garage business in the yard behind, and then a butchers shop. To our left the main street continued to a bakery, a grocer, then Mrs. Jones' little sweet shop, the post office and the chemist before reaching the crossroads by the Star Inn, with the saddler and the Co-Op on the Gloucester street, the greengrocer and another garage on the Cheltenham road.

Opposite the church stood a residential hotel, to its left the Baptist church. Then came the filling station and a chain branch grocer, followed by the very important bicycle shop where torch batteries could sometimes be bought, and where those with battery operated wireless sets took their accumulator batteries for re-charging. Just beyond, on the narrowest part of the main street was the entrance to the builders yard, where also lived the red fire engine.

In the middle of the junction opposite our house a stone pedestal carried a fine wrought standard lantern, and past it the street running away from the main road led to the cobbler, another baker, the dairy, the police station and public baths, and then to another junction where stood Lizzie Clark's little hardware store, supplier of firewood bundles, paraffin and firefighters. Hereabouts too were the newsagent, another butcher, the Roman Catholic church, two more pubs, and finally our coal merchant.

That was not quite all the village even in those days, but it was as much as we two little strangers could learn in the few weeks before the clocks changed. Of course the village was not just buildings, but people as well; it was going to be a long time before we began to know any of them.

The war was very remote from us, we heard that our soldiers were fighting in France, and of one group or another locally being called up, but it conveyed no message to our young minds. But all these local folk knew how their sons, husbands and neighbours were going away in their heavy wool serge uniforms, and they knew all the doubt and fear for their safety. They closed ranks to keep the home fires burning. News only came from the papers or by the wireless, and grown-ups knew well that such information would be incomplete, and slanted to keep up home morale.

The first big news of the autumn was reported, and was very bad. In our own naval anchorage at Scapa Flow the battleship *Royal Oak* was torpedoed, and sank with the loss of eight hundred and ten crew. Adults were very quiet and solemn, prayers at school included this terrible event, but I could make no computation of this great figure, nearly three times the number of boys in the school, and what did dead mean anyway? There was just a hint, I felt, that the fact that this sinking had been accomplished was even more horrifying than the casualty total.

There were, as I have said, two grocers, two butchers and two bakers in the village, and with rationing soon coming choices had to be made. Every housewife, mother included, was required to register with a supplier, not simply for the ration when the time came, but because shopkeepers naturally favoured their registered customers when they had stock of some item in short supply. The result was that one butcher, one baker and one grocer never had our custom, admirable providers though they were.

The noise of battle had not reached us but the warbling note of the air-raid alert was frequently practised, followed a few minutes later by a continuous tone for the all-clear signal. Both in Stroud and at Painswick there was urgent need for sandbags to be filled, and even small boys such as ourselves were welcome to help. Frequently we returned from school having missed one or two buses, our navy gaberdine raincoats well spattered with yellow sand. Filling the bags soon lost its excitement, but I could have watched for hours as the skilled adults with their big leather palms stitched up the bags to close the end using a wicked looking curved needle. Gradually important buildings and air-raid shelters grew their anti-blast protection walls of sandbags. In the next year or so many strange things were done for the purposes of war.

There came horrid destruction, and I simply had to watch, though my eyes hurt. A lorry arrived, and a trolley carrying two gas cylinders, and I was introduced to the wonders of oxy-acetylene flame cutting through iron, as all the fine railings around the village were felled. Spitting sparks which rolled along the pavement as tiny iron balls were a noisy firework display, no wonder the man operating the cutter wore a great leather apron, gauntlets and goggles. I was too young to bleed over the loss of so much fine craftsmanship, it was just another odd happening in this time of unfamiliar occurrences.

Novelty took another step when we were asked to collect horse-chestnuts to feed to pigs. Now even I knew that conkers were poisonous, but we joined in the gathering of bagfuls and sackfuls which all eventually accompanied us on the school bus to the collection point.

More threatening sights appeared. Concrete pillboxes were built at corners of lanes, patterns of covered holes in roads marked sites for obstructions to be inserted if the enemy came, and drums filled with concrete were grouped at narrow spots where they could be quickly moved to hamper an advance.

Such memories remain from a period when little of great moment affected us. School offered little excitement, more especially as we could not see out of the windows during lessons, and it was a very wearisome business carrying all ones personal possessions, textbooks and exercise books to and from school every day because the Handsworth boys used the desks in the afternoon. The double decker buses were cold, even after the last of the type with curving outside stairways had gone, the draught from the open boarding platform at the back successfully competed with the new whirring fan heaters at the front of both decks.

Life became a matter of getting dressed in the morning as late as possible, swallow the hot porridge just as the school bus appeared, then take the swollen satchel with its gymnastic or games kit and sandwiches, not to mention the necessary books and writing materials, and nip across the road as the bus was about to leave. By late afternoon we were back, with scarcely a thought for how mother had kept the house warm or done her other jobs.

We had no maid now, but mother knew how to keep house and she stoked, shopped, dusted, laundered, swept and most importantly cooked to keep us all warm and comfortable on our return. Childrens Hour on the wireless was permitted listening, and then after our hot meal the table was cleared and our bit of homework was done before we returned again to the front sitting room where the wireless lived. Reading soon became a favourite pastime, a benefit that has remained with us ever since. Scarcely graduated from our Blackie readers we would in the next year or so become avid readers of really exciting boys books.

Mother too enjoyed reading in the evenings, but more frequently she would be darning our socks. Her day started very early, riddling the anthracite boiler which she hoped had stayed alight overnight, then lighting the open fire in the front room. The breakfast laid, she then brought cups of hot tea to us, and made our lunch sandwiches.

Once we had breakfasted and left for school she made the beds, aired the bedrooms, washed up, and did the shopping up the village street. Sometimes the bus to Stroud would take her to a wider range of stores and to Boots subscription library where she could change her books.

Then there was the washing to do, all of it by hand, though the sheets now went into a gas heated boiler. For the rest it was hot water in the stoneware sink, the water softened with washing soda, then the clothes scrubbed with bar soap on the scrubbing board, then rinsed and twisted to get out most of the water. We no longer had the great iron framed mangle with its wooden rollers that had stayed in London, now a lighter weight Acme wringer with rubber rollers, which clamped onto a trestle with a bowl beneath did the same job of getting the water out of clothes between the nip rollers. Woollens alone received gentler treatment, soaking in a bowl of Lux flakes suds, followed by rinsing and gentle hand wringing.

This was not very kind to hands, but I never remember seeing her use rubber gloves, though she did use cotton ones when polishing the silver. That was to protect the silver of course. The table knives too had to be polished on a long board set with leather strips dusted with polishing powder; the result dangerously sharp sheer steel blades.

There were doorsteps to be scoured, carpets swept, mats shaken, furniture dusted, washing dried and ironed, we lads kept fed and tidy; and all the time on the near horizon loomed Friday.

The Cheltenham Flyer from Paddington on Friday evening brought father to Stroud, then a local hire car delivered him to Painswick, where we all waited anxiously, hoping that our preparations had left nothing to annoy him. The Monday morning Flyer would take him back to Town, meanwhile we sat on the edge of our seats so to speak. Times were difficult in the world of grown-ups which we so little understood, and mother kept her household cash book meticulously made up to the last farthing all her days.

Sunday lunch however still remained something to look forward to. The sirloin might not be quite so large, but the roast potatoes and Yorkshire pudding were still perfect, with wonderful hot sweets such as spotted dick or treacle sponge to follow generously sauced with thick creamy custard.

As usual the pre-Christmas pudding and mincemeat making took place, though the ingredients must have involved mother in a good deal of seeking, and the sight of all these preparations put young boys in their accustomed fever of anticipation.

Then suddenly the war news became exciting again. I knew that fighting had continued on land and sea over the past months, but the story that now caught the imagination was of the pursuit of a German pocket-battleship right down into the south Atlantic where it eventually took refuge with its escorts in the neutral port of Montevideo to make repairs to battle damage.

Having overstayed the time allowed under neutrality rules the *Graf Spee* sailed out and was scuttled. It was a nice news boost for Christmas.

Daylight was now gone by half past four and the blackout rules meant that there could be no church services in the evening, and any knock on the front door required first that one pick up the little torch, next turn off the hall light, and only then open the door, trying to recognise the caller with the torch beam still downwards.

Until the end of school term this left our little jobs to Saturday afternoon and Sunday. Grey woollen gloves and black wellingtons with our school raincoats protected our twig gathering expeditions as the days became shorter. With a hessian sack each we walked up the Gloucester road to the Plantation which bounded the westward side of the lower slopes of Painswick beacon. Despite warm clothing it was a chilly business filling those sacks with fallen twigs, each having to be broken into short lengths to pack the sack. All the time the weather was becoming colder, and our fingers were stinging by the time we had carried our load back home.

Keeping ourselves warm became our main preoccupation, keeping the home warm was mother's task but we helped with filling fuel hods and buckets. The passage running right through the house provided ample draught for open fires in the rooms off, but the heat went up the chimney for the most part. Draw your chair up to the fire to warm hands and toes and the reward was a cold back and chilblains. Throw a rug against the bottom of the door to reduce the draught and the fire would soon be sulking. It was difficult to find the best arrangement.

Plenty of woollen underwear and thick jerseys were the order of the day; wool blankets, hot water bottles and thick pyjamas the bedtime rig. But in between, a couple of times a week came bathtime. The hot water boiler did a good job, but the upstairs rooms were very chilly and undressing demanded great haste and a sprint to the bath. Basking briefly in the steaming hot water, there followed the quickest of towelling down before peeling our pyjamas from around the hot water bottle and climbing into the warm part of the bed before the bathwater cooled.

Christmas was different in so many ways. Our little living room could not compare with the big double drawing room we had left behind, front windows displayed no lighted Christmas trees, there were no relatives to call on us or visits to be made. On a reduced scale however there were little family festivities, our stockings still contained happy surprises.

It had been cold enough before Christmas, but as we returned to school early in January 1940 the weather became colder still, and everybody had a constant struggle to prevent water systems freezing. Overflows grew long icicles, as did split pipes, and ice became a constant hazard on pavements. Mother spent hours pouring kettles of hot water over the hessian lagging on our outdoor pipes. Villagers long accustomed to the problems of winter bound their shoes in sacking to walk along the street. School buses managed to keep going and magnificent rink-like slides appeared on school play grounds. It was from the homeward school bus that we one day saw the product of the icy road surface, where a lorry from Townsends the cattle feed makers had crashed over the wall and down the bank into the Washbrook at the bottom of Painswick Hill. Broken cattle cake discs lay everywhere. Within a few minutes of our arrival at home a stream of folk could be seen rushing down the hill with trolleys, prams, wheelbarrows, buckets and sacks to gather the bounty strewn beside the road. They soon tidied it all up; most of the village families kept a few chickens and this sort of gift was not to be wasted.

    Then strangely, after weeks of hard frost with no thaw in prospect it started to rain. Steady rather than heavy rain, small droplets driven on a light east wind froze instantly on landing. The east facing front wall of our house was soon glazed with ice; so too were the roads, and on tree branches, power cables, telephone lines and even blades of grass the ice built up until it was a thick coat of immense weight.

    Walking in the long grass on the hill to admire this strange spectacle we crunched along through stems as thick as sticks of seaside rock that tinkled as we pushed through them. All along the windward side of the wood great beech boughs were weighed down by the ice, often as thick as the branch on which it had formed; and with frightening crashes one tree after another split off a great piece to fall for next year's firewood. On the hillside haystacks looked as if made of glass, so thick was the ice layer covering them. From a domestic standpoint the real worry concerned telephone wires and power cables, and everybody watched anxiously as they got fatter and fatter and lower and lower.

The electricity supply to our house came from a large distribution pole on the other side of the street to a bracket mounted on the wall of our house above the first floor front bedroom window. Late one night came the inevitable flash and a loud bang, and we were without electricity, the entire bracket having ripped away from the wall. We were of course only one household in thousands with the same problem, and it was some days before we once again put the candles aside for reserve use. Fortunately we used electricity for little else than lighting, and a few days with candles seemed just another change one had to put up with if you swapped town living for a country home. For all we knew this sort of freeze-up might be an annual event on these hills. Not being party to adult conversation we had not heard that it was at that time unique in living memory, nor could we guess that in the next fifty years we would see no repetition of this terribly destructive glazed frost.

Force of circumstance was giving us more independence. Mother could not possibly run a home and keep us constantly under her eye. As a result we began to explore the near vicinity of our home in what was the beginning of our real education. We were surrounded by new and fascinating sights. When the inevitable thaw eventually arrived, and the last of the snow disappeared we found to our great astonishment that actually beneath the snow blanket little white flowers had grown, and banks of snowdrops dotted the dark wet ground among last year's rotting leaves. It was a wonderful discovery and we took a bunch home for mother.

The hedgerows were still bare, their small bird population readily visible, and we quickly became aware of the many different shapes, colours and sizes they took. A pocket bird book and a wildflower book in the same series soon became well thumbed.

At school the strange routine resumed and life continued on a fairly dull plane while the short evenings lasted. We looked forward to the time when we could play in daylight after tea. Meanwhile the war news was bad; or so we gathered from the little we heard on the wireless. It was, I now realise, a time of military disaster culminating at the end of May in the recovery of 338,000 men from the beaches of Dunkirk. My young mind could not encompass the meaning of this, but our world was full of serious faces, and Sunday 26th May had been a National Day of Prayer. I could not remember one of those before. People seemed to feel that the land war could come to us, and menfolk too old for active service started enrolling in the Local Defence Volunteers.

# CHAPTER 4

I did not look forward to the longer days so far as school life was concerned. My intense shyness often left me incapable of answering a question, and in the previous autumn I had been the victim of some nasty bullying. On one occasion I had been waylaid outside the school gates by three large fourth formers, and followed my mother's instruction never to retaliate or resist lest a harder fate befall. When I arrived home she was alarmed to find me completely deaf. Examination showed that my ears had been plugged with putty.

The doctor removed the putty and mother interviewed the headmaster the following day. I could not say a word about the attack and was far too frightened to identify my assailants. Father was told and lengthened his weekend to interview the headmaster on the following Monday. I believe the staff could guess the identity of the culprits but could do nothing while I maintained my silence. I took to waiting until most boys had left for home after school before making a dash to the canal towpath which ran roughly parallel to the road to Stroud, then catching a bus from the town centre. As the days shortened so the risk of attack had seemed to reduce, people were too busy trying to get home before dark to worry about me.

But now the lighter evenings had returned and I was worried lest this skinny little chap with the posh London accent might once again attract predators. Again the towpath by the old canal became my homeward route to Stroud, and now it was becoming really interesting. Moorhens, coots and ducks were rearing families, water voles and rats were enjoying the new reed growth and in the case of the rats a feast of eggs. The dead dark water of the winter now showed clear with tadpoles, newts and sticklebacks among the growing weed. One sunny day I had paused to watch them, sitting on the stone abutment of the little swing bridge at the bottom of Murder Lane, and paid the price for not guarding my rear. I was picked up unceremoniously by the four corners and thrown into the canal. Nearly all its width was a mass of reeds, and there I landed, with a very muddy struggle to get out. The last yard to the bank was far the worst part, a bed of keen young nettles which left my bare knees red for a long time.

Fortunately that was the last time I was attacked, and the natural history of that canal bank and its reed beds became a growing interest before my horizons expanded to the surrounding hills. First however it was necessary to develop a keen habit of constantly lifting the eyes beyond the hills, to the sky above and the aircraft which increasingly flew over. Through the winter grown-ups and children alike had studied aircraft recognition books which showed silhouettes of British and German planes, in head-on view, as seen from below and as viewed from the side. So far British aircraft only had appeared, Gloucester Gladiators, and the occasional Hurricane or Spitfire. Twin engined Airspeed Oxfords and Avro Ansons often flew over, but the enemy had not yet arrived.

We had settled into our new surroundings now and were ready to look at the countryside around. Our London experience had been limited, so far as day-to-day life was concerned, to brick built streets, small public parks, a generally fairly level district where there were consequently no extensive views. Now we looked out from our lofty perch in Painswick's main street across a beautiful green valley patchworked with hedgerows and dotted with pale Cotswold stone cottages and little farmsteads away to the long beechwood topping the opposite hill. The network of lanes and footpaths clearly visible across the valley would enable us to extend our exploration as spring approached.

Everywhere our outings taught us flowers. From that first magic of the snowdrops opening as the snow melted came a succession of revelations as the dark banks of the sunken lanes came alive again with violets, primroses, wood anemones and bluebells. Mother always welcomed our offerings, but we quickly learned that some flowers soon collapsed when picked. Not yet venturing into the pasture fields we watched as they became masses of cowslips, milkmaids and other flowers of every type and colour, before the grass grew taller and it was time to cut the hay.

Big horses pulled rattling mowers round and round the field until all the grass was laid low. A few days later a line of men and lads could be seen throwing the hay up with pitchforks to turn it over, and we noted carefully a task where we might one day be allowed to be useful. Then came the big horse again pulling a great wide rake with curving forward pointed tines. As it was hauled along the rake gradually filled with the drying hay, and the driver pulled a lever to drop the load. Repeating the process around the field left neat lines of hay in windrows for the final drying. The last job brought the men and lads back again as several horse-drawn carts arrived and the boys pitchforked the hay up to their seniors on the carts who packed it down to be carried to the stack where it was once more tossed up to the rick builders on the top. Truly fascinating this, it demanded several dry days and then a sunny one for the stacking. Consequently we remembered it as another job we would like to do when we were old enough. Watching from a distance we did not learn the less attractive side of haymaking, the myriad tiny biting insects which left you covered in red spots when the job was done.

Meanwhile the hedgerows had come into leaf and produced masses of hawthorn flowers with their heavy perfume attracting flies and bees. Amongst that leaf cover birds were nesting, and we soon realised how much easier it was to spot a little nest looking upward into a hedge from the bottom of a sunken lane, than when the hedge was on the same level as the observer. But where tall trees bounded the lane and the rooks had colonised their tops we moved on quickly. Apart from the constant noise of the calling rooks, the road was liberally sprinkled with droppings, pieces of twig and numerous dead chicks. We never did find out how those chicks came to be pushed out of their nests, I suppose we just did not stay long enough.

Sometimes we would meet the local lengthman whose task it was to keep the lanes tidy. With his barrow, shovel and hook he worked his way round the village trimming the grass banks and keeping the soakaway gullies clear of soil. He always had a smile for us, and I often thought what a enviable job he had, never far from home, in the middle of all that lovely countryside. He always seemed to know every nest in the hedges.

At school the summer brought a novel addition to the routine. Gym and games I hated, only because I had to take all my clothes off in public which always made me most acutely embarrassed. Now however came a time when we went to the new open-air swimming pool at Stratford park for swimming lessons. Here at least we undressed in cubicles rather than the great open changing room at school. It involved quite a rush to complete the five minute run to the pool and the return trip, changing, towelling down and dressing, and still leave some lesson time for instruction. I quite enjoyed it, and later that summer visited the pool on several sunny days. Entry for youngsters cost only three pence and my season ticket meant the bus travel was free. Sometimes there was enough money for a custard coloured ice-cream which had to be eaten very quickly before it dissolved in sticky drips.

With the coming of summer the war was at last getting closer, until one day the air raid sirens sounded, we heard some distant explosions, and were told later that some bombs had been dropped to the south of our district. Out came the aircraft recognition books again, with the war so depressing since the Dunkirk evacuation a German attack seemed the obvious sequel.

There came a lovely summer afternoon, sunny with lumps of cauliflower cloud floating high in a clear blue sky. It must have been about a quarter to two in the afternoon, for I was sitting on the warm concrete steps of the school pavilion eating my sandwich lunch. From where I sat the cricket fields stretched away southward to the main road, beyond lay the rugby field, and then the dip to the valley floor and the old canal. In the distance the hillside rose, built up towards Rodborough to the leftward, while to the right the green expanse of Selsley common gave the skyline.

I watched a Gloucester Gladiator appear, climbing steeply as was their speciality, then puffs of smoke began to show near one of the clouds, but having never seen anti-aircraft fire before it was a moment or two before I recognised it.

Then suddenly a twin engined aircraft entered my field of view flying fast from the west about a hundred feet above the line of the canal, and almost on my eye level. Memory did its stuff, JU88 I immediately realised, thus so incredibly close my first sight of an enemy aircraft.

But this was certainly not the plane up in that cloud, a Hurricane and a Spitfire were now sniffing around to flush that one out. I must be honest and admit that I did not see that plane shot down, but indeed it was on the afternoon of Thursday 25th July as the records confirm. The one I saw apparently got away, for accounts of the day speak of three enemy aircraft in the area at the time.

I remember no raid warning, but with hindsight this was a timely reminder of the much more dangerous phase that now began. Bombing raids on the Severn vale towns became frequent, and the principal danger to everyone in our area was soon recognised as the shower of jagged steel fragments known as shrapnel which came down when an anti-aircraft shell exploded. Get indoors quickly and stay there was the answer. Those horrid bits of metal could sometimes be heard rattling down the roof tiles at night, and lay on roads and pavements in the morning. I feel sure they must have damaged many a lawnmower as they would have buried themselves partly in the turf to snag the mower blade later.

Until now our local exploration had been confined to the visible valley to the east of Painswick, we had not yet visited the other on the westward side of the spur with the village of Edge on its opposite hill. The great drop to the Severn valley with all its potential bombing targets and the groupings of observation, anti-aircraft and searchlight units which now lined the edge of the scarp, remained beyond our knowledge.

We were vaguely aware that there were several military aerodromes in the area, and that there was an aircraft factory near Gloucester, but at the age of nine my knowledge of local geography was very flimsy. So incomplete was it in fact that when all the direction signposts around our countryside were taken down, as they were that autumn in order not to assist an invader, they made no difference to me since in our wanderings we simply navigated by the sight of that big village on the hill to which we must eventually return.

Shortly after my encounter with the JU88 came the end of term, holidays abroad or at the seaside were out of the question of course, but our countryside surroundings still held plenty of novelty to keep us occupied. I was beginning to feel slightly less shy and overawed at school, and looked forward to the new term when, with most of my class, we would find ourselves moved up to form one.

Meanwhile our horizons slowly extended, and beyond the wood on the west side of Painswick beacon we found a fascinating expanse of tumbled ground thickly grown with young fir trees. It was a perfect place for hiding and seeking games, for stalking and for building dens. Other lads living toward the top of the village also played there and soon we were part of a group of half a dozen or so who would take it in turns to climb a tree whilst the rest disappeared before trying to return to the tree before the climber spotted them. Pine branches almost touching the ground and long dry grass made undetected approach very difficult. Without realising it we were learning fieldcraft, silent movement using cover, which was basic to any close view of the countryside and its wildlife, besides being of great importance if we ever had to serve in the army. There had been a few air raids, and we had heard exploding bombs in the distance, but we felt fairly safe among these overgrown quarry spoil heaps, after all we were out of sight and could run back almost the whole way to the village without breaking cover should the need arise.

The short summer holiday over, I now found my classroom on the opposite side of the main school hall. Last year our windows had faced into the enclosed quadrangle, with three lines of buildings shielding us from the sounds of the railway. Now we looked out across the cricket fields with an uninterrupted view of the main line with its frequent and varied traffic. Great Western railway passenger trains in chocolate and cream livery were hauled by big green steam engines with gold lining. They passed at only moderate speed for Stroud was only a mile away where they stopped. Goods trains hauled by less smart engines seemed to go on rattling past interminably, some of the coal trains pulling over sixty trucks and a guard's van at the back with open rear platform. In addition a local service between the many halts in the Stroud valley was provided by smart new diesel rail-cars with a distinctive warning hooter quite different from the shrill steam whistle of the locomotives. Many of my contemporaries started collecting the names or numbers of engines, a hobby which some continued for years.

Just as I was beginning to feel less of an oddity at school my social integration suffered a horrid setback. I had developed a swollen gland in the left side of my neck and it would not subside. The doctors decided that this was caused by bovine tuberculosis. I was told that the problem with this condition was that a blow on another part of the body could produce other swollen glands; a kick on the shin for example threatening a swollen gland behind the shin bone. It was further felt that I needed building up, I was after all a skinny little chap, and I must henceforth drink a pint of full-cream milk every day. Milk drinking totally revolted me and so huge jars of Horlicks were prescribed to make it a bit more tolerable. Our delicious winter tonic of cod liver oil and malt suddenly changed, so far as I was concerned, when the doctor wrote on the prescription 'MOP'. That translated by the pharmacist meant 'malt and oil and Parrish's Chemical Food' an iron and mineral addition to our favourite treacly tonic which turned it black, made it taste of rusty nails, and left my teeth and tongue black too. Up at the hospital an attempt was made using a very big needle to suck out the contents of my swelling. Rather painfully it failed and for the next couple of years I had to put up with pulling zinc oxide plasters off the oozing wound every day.

I must not attend school for an entire term, and when I returned I would not be allowed to do gym, cricket or rugby, nor to use the swimming pool at Stratford park. These prohibitions were to be permanent. Meanwhile I must attend the outpatient department at Stroud hospital twice a week for ultra-violet ray treatment.

The prospect of school with no gym, games or swimming was very depressing, I seemed doomed to a continuing lonely existence when I returned, but first I had to get through that term at home. A certain amount of school work was brought home for me, and duly completed, but I had to get out of the house as much as possible to flee mother's constant attention. I took to walking the three miles to Stroud and up the hill to the hospital. There I was told to strip to my underpants and lie under the ultra-violet tubes with very dark goggles to protect my eyes. The session over I dressed and went down to the public library. There I selected three books and walked back to Painswick with them. Three days later, with my next hospital treatment due, I had finished reading those books and returned them to the library on my way back from the hospital, choosing three more before walking home again.

It was a simple routine which only varied if there was heavy rain, my bus season ticket was still in the pocket of my mackintosh if needed. I had never done so much reading, but it proved valuable experience when I came to examination years later on. I sampled many different types of book, fiction for the most part, seafaring stories, exploration adventures, fantasy such as Gulliver's Travels and Arabian Nights, the flying exploits of Biggles and the adventures of Huckleberry Finn. Just as interesting and exciting were books on motor racing in the pre-war years, I read every one of these that the library could provide.

I felt that I was still spending too much time in the house, I needed an outdoor pastime away from home. Inspired perhaps by Huckleberry Finn I decided to take up fishing to get some peace and quiet. Many times I had peered over the stonework below Wallbridge lock on the old canal at Stroud, watching the little sticklebacks as they cruised in and out of the water weed. They would have to do for a start. I tied a length of thread to the end of a slim garden cane, then with an empty jam jar and a small slice of bread I caught the bus to Stroud. At Edmunds' shop in Gloucester street I bought the smallest hook they had, a size fourteen. This came as a tiny hook tied to a short length of fine gut, all coiled in a little transparent paper envelope. I also bought a very small quill float.

Down below the lock I threaded up my float, tied my hook beneath and hid its point in a bit of bread crust. Lowering the bait carefully into the water I watched as the sticklebacks approached the slowly sinking crust and started nibbling it from various directions quite enthusiastically. It was soon obvious that this was a good way of feeding fish, but not of catching them, the bait was far too large. A piece of bread dough, slightly damped and squeezed hard enabled me to pinch off a tiny bit rather smaller than a pin head. This I put right on the point of the hook, and watched as it lowered into the water. So small a bait did not attract the hungry crowd my earlier offering had brought, but the fish were still there, and soon one came along to look at my speck of dough. He took it and I caught him, my first success with rod and line. Four others followed him into my jam jar, and then it was time to go home with the evidence of my success. The colder autumn days approaching discouraged further expeditions that year, but an interest had been born which would become a major component of my leisure activities for many years to come.

The war seemed to be getting much closer to us. The wireless spoke of heavy raids on London, Bristol too was being hit hard. On one or two evenings after dark we walked along Edge Lane to look out towards Bristol over the big Dry Knapps field. Far away we could see searchlight beams and great flashes as bombs exploded. At our apparently safe distance the life of two small boys transplanted so abruptly from town to country continued much as that of the indigenous youngsters of the village.

We had by now reached the stage where the vital tool was a knife. Toys were discarded in favour of tools, and each year our first choice for a Christmas present was a better knife. Our first little penknives were not robust enough to cut sticks, and it was sticks which now made our toys. We had noticed how hazel bushes sprouted a lot of straight slim sticks from the base, which would grow to nearly ten feet, by which time the base was an inch thick. It needed a sharp stout blade to cut through that thickness. In fact we cut through these sticks with knives which were both flimsy and blunt, enthusiasm providing the extra effort needed. With the thin end cut off short of branching twigs and the heavy end pointed this was a spear. Our exploration had taken us now as far as Painswick park, where we could exercise our throwing arms without risk to anybody.

Those spears had another use. We were intensely attracted to water, whether the local brook, a pond, or some tiny rivulet, and we had soon learned that between firm ground and water there was almost always mud. Probing with spears showed whether the mud would come over our little wellingtons and whether the water was too deep for wading. A book I had been reading told how marsh gas could be collected by holding a water filled jam jar upside down in a pond or brook while stirring the mud immediately beneath with a stick. The bubbles caught in the jar would eventually fill it. Lift out the jar, turn it upright and apply a lighted match and the gas burned with a pretty blue flame. If on the other hand you blew gently into the top of the jar before lighting, the match would produce a loud pop. We played this little game several times down at the bottom of Edge lane in the Washbrook.

As winter approached flocks of small birds appeared in the leafless hedgerows and with our pocket handbooks we could now recognise the different tits, especially the delightful long tailed tit which tended to flock separately from the finches, blue tits, great tits and coal tits, and to be even more restless. I may have been missing a bit of school, but we were both acquiring knowledge of our environment at a great rate. There was not a single experience which did not leave its mark in memory.

Quiet Christmas came and went, subdued of course by the black-out. Two enormous explosions a mile or two away a few weeks earlier had underlined the absolute need to prevent any light from showing at night. But now we had at least been given our magnificent new knives and could face the opportunities of the countryside with keen anticipation. The Bushman's Friend was a wood handled sheath knife with big brass rivets sharing a leather sheath with a matching sharpening steel. It really looked most impressive. Only later were we to find that the steel did not sharpen the blade, merely putting a burr on it, and that the blade was too flimsy for the job in that it was the same thickness throughout. Thus in time we learned to look for a blade with a good stout back to it.

Before we had a chance to try out our new tools a great blanket of snow descended. As it drifted up against the doors and windows the house seemed warmer as the draught gaps became blocked. Outside people walked up and down the street on silent feet.

Wheeled traffic almost completely disappeared. There was little enough at any time apart from delivery lorries and the infrequent buses; few people owned cars and fewer still had a petrol allowance. Doctors and magistrates were among the exceptions. For some days hardly any tyres came to compact the snow, and villagers took to pulling their bit of shopping along on sledges.

We had seen sledges in use the previous winter when the village boys pulled theirs up onto the beacon to one of the two favourite runs. The valley green, in reality the fifteenth hole of the dormant golf club, was a teardrop shaped depression about a hundred yards long beside the upper part of the plantation. Falling steadily towards the wider end, and with steep banks and small pines along one side it offered enough excitement for smaller people such as ourselves.

The other sledge run was far longer and faster. The first fairway of the golf course was known as the cemetery run, principally because it ran parallel to the boundary wall of the cemetery. Fairly steep, the grass closely cut, sledges quickly reached a speed sufficient to take off each time they struck one of the shallow dips that crossed their line in several places. At the bottom came an abrupt finish, a roadway followed by the wall surrounding the clubhouse. That sledge had to be smartly turned or the rider had to roll off before they struck the wall. There was a third alternative for the very daring. A narrow wicket gate in the wall, barely wider than a sledge gave onto a few steps down to the gravelled area around the clubhouse. This gate was propped open and a very few tried to steer through it. Approaching at about twenty miles per hour headfirst and steering with the touch of a foot or gloved fingertips, the decision to try for the gate was a last moment business, and if the sledge hit a gatepost the rider was catapulted straight down the steps onto the gravel beyond. At least the sledge would be twisted, at worst broken. As for the rider it gave another possible meaning to the cemetery run.

The valley green was quite sufficient for us at present, and as last year we had no sledge. The village boys had home-made sledges, produced by fathers or elder brothers. So far as we were concerned father was not there, nor was he noted for using saw or hammer and nails. He was used to using tradesmen for that sort of thing. Some few people had the high spar built toboggans of the Davos type, but there was no question of buying one. What we wanted was the ordinary low board platform with a pair of sturdy wooden runners, the best of which were shod with strip iron. We simply could not spend another winter hanging shyly around valley green in the hope that somebody would offer us a go on their sledge.

In an outhouse we found some old bits of planking, and a wooden box with a small saw, a claw hammer, brace and bit and a few other oddments of tools which had come down from London. With these my brother built a sledge, and a bit of the spare length of mother's washing line provided the pulling rope. We hauled it up to the valley green, but it was not a great success. The snow was so deep that year that whilst it could be pulled along readily enough, the weight of a rider made it plough into the snow. Where others had been before and the surface was compacted it ran better, but lacking iron runners was slow and difficult to steer. It was however a start, and told us what improvements were needed.

Meanwhile in January 1941 I was going back to school, and that strange regime of six half days a week. On some snowy mornings the bus did not arrive, and at a quarter past eight somebody telephoned to find out whether or not it was on its way.

Some thirty or so of us from the Stroud schools had waited, rubbing hands and stamping feet to try to keep warm, and if at last we heard that the bus could not get through there came a moment for instant decision. A few turned away to walk home, but the rest started to walk the four miles to school. In fact the thought of all that traffic-free road, starting down the big Painswick hill was a marvellous stimulus after hanging about for the bus, and big and small ran hard, sliding where the snow was packed, until we all arrived rather blown at the bottom of the hill and settled to a fast walk. This was not the sort of convoy that moved at the speed of the slowest, rather the bigger lads herded the smaller, giving a helping pull where necessary. Girls too adopted the same system and we all trooped along, stretched across the width of the road, ruddy faced by the exertion and the cold morning.

We earned no medals, for we were not alone. From most of the area served by our schools few failed to turn up due to weather, and many had a harder journey than the Painswick group.

The cold weather continued, and each new fall of snow added to the interest. We had seen all the common birds, but apart from rabbits and the occasional squirrel the wild animals of the countryside kept out of sight. Probably we had not yet learned enough to find foxes and badgers. But a new cover of snow, however light, showed all manner of footprints and tracks until the sun got to work. It was time now for another reference pocketbook, and the start of another accumulation of knowledge. We began to tell dog from fox and fox from badger by their footprints. Many years and many track sightings later, and without much further reference to the book one can almost tell the age, sex and health of, for example, a fox by a few footprints.

At last the snow cleared and on the beacon the cold east wind dried out all the dead grass of last year. Along the sides of the golf fairways the old grass was being burned. The turf beneath was cold and damp, and the strong wind rushed the fire along so fast that though the ash coated the new grass black until the next rain, the plants and snails came to no harm.

One bright cold morning we had walked up to the top of the slope beyond our summer hide-and-seek play area to the last rise before the beacon itself. Ahead the short grass shone bright green, but to our left matt black ground stretched down towards the edge of the small pine trees. Quietly exploring this ash covered slope, with its old snail shells and the remains of last years' field mouse nests, something odd caught my eye. Where the slightly scorched end of a little pine branch touched the steep black bank there was a small ginger coloured object. We approached very quietly and found what appeared to be a tiny brown kitten with great big eyes and long ears held down along its back. It was a baby hare, a leveret and the first we had ever seen.

Not knowing then that hares sometimes hide their young in different places around their territory we picked the little thing up, and putting it in a snug mackintosh pocket we carried it carefully home to mother. Fortunately she knew that the sisters who ran the pub a few doors down the street kept rabbits and had reared wild ones. They took our little orphan in, and over the next few years there grew a big handsome hare which lived in an extra large hutch of its own beside the rabbit hutches in the yard. We were later told that it became sufficiently tame to run around in the private part of the house, but was never allowed in the public rooms. I have seen many hares over the years, but oddly enough have never encountered another leveret, so that lovely silky long-eared kitten keeps a very special place in memory.

It seemed as if the bad weather had kept the bombers away, as soon as it improved they returned and the Bristol area appeared all too often to be ablaze against the night sky. We were barely conscious of the situation however, or of the progress of the war; our principal interest concerned rationing, and the shortage of other necessities. There was talk of getting help from the Americans, but just what they would provide nobody knew.

Home from school we took our knives and spears to the park once more. Near the old pigeon house was a thicket of brambles and hazel, and this time we intended to make bows and arrows from the slim hazel shafts. First however we spotted that the little muddy pond below was a mass of frogs, crawling slowly around in the weedy mud, each large frog with a smaller one riding piggy back. It was surprising how tough the skin of those frogs was, but we were able to satisfy ourselves that our spears really were fairly sharp.

We cut two stout hazel sticks for bows and a number of smaller ones for arrows and took them home, where we bent the bows to stout string and cut points on the thicker ends of the arrows. Flights were a problem, the flight end of the arrow had to be notched to take the bowstring, but if you split it to take a rook feather flight the split then needed tight binding to keep the notch closed. We managed after a fashion, and had quite a lot of fun loosing arrows at trees and thistles as we wandered the fields.

Following my efforts with the sticklebacks my brother too had decided to take up fishing, and on one of his lone forays beyond the brow of Bulls Cross had found a promising pond. We went back to have a closer look. Down the steep lane from the village, up to the top of the opposite hill, and then all the way down into the bottom of the next valley, the last descent by a very worn and washed out stone road. At the bottom a little tarmac lane crossed our path, and just to the right we could see willows and reeds beside the road. Very quietly we approached, but the moorhens spotted us and retired quickly to cover. The pond was roughly triangular, the roadward side impossible to fish from due to trees and reeds. The other long side was guarded by the stream, flowing in a separate channel beside the pond. The third short side was different. This was in fact an old man-made dam carrying a stone track which brought the cows from the hillside pasture back to the low stone cowsheds of the farm below the dam. Here were no reeds or trees to obstruct the fisherman, the edge of the water only a yard from the track. The only problem was that underfoot lay an ever fresh mixture of churned mud and cow dung. It was of course a perfect boys pond. Nobody else would be likely to want to compete for whatever fish it contained for there was no boat. Having found out that we would be allowed to fish we went home.

We were left with the question of where to get fishing rods, but that had to wait a little while because we were right in the midst of the bird nesting season. We had obtained two old wooden collecting boxes with plush lined compartments and webbing shoulder strap and now started to form our collections of eggs. Blackbirds and thrushes were easy, their egg colours clearly differing, besides which the mud lined nest of the thrush could not be mistaken for the grassy blackbird nest. Robins' nests were better hidden, and some finches' eggs would only be collected in later years, their nests too high for us yet. At the price of mud filled wellingtons we acquired moorhen eggs, but we found no mallard nests that first collecting season. All these specimens had to have a small hole pierced in each end, and the contents blown out to leave an empty shell. It could be a messy business, especially if the egg we had chosen had been laid some time earlier.

# CHAPTER 5

So far as I was concerned matters seemed to be taking a turn for the better. I had to stand behind the wallbars during gym, but despite my long absence I did not feel such a stranger in class. Then one day a new sound arose from the railway line, as of a big engine struggling with a very heavy load, and suddenly it sounded its whistle. This was like no whistle we had ever heard, except in an American film. The great twin tone blast made my hair stand on end, the Americans had arrived. They had not of course, but this was our first sight of the big grey locomotives that the lend-lease arrangement provided, to become a familiar sight for the rest of the war and beyond hauling freight and war materials.

Then there was the man over the wall. In London neither we nor our parents had had any contact with our neighbours, this being the normal custom. Now in Painswick the system continued, helped by the way our house was constructed. On the uphill side the adjoining large house had a high boundary wall on our side stretching half way up the back garden. We could have no view of the ground floor whatever. Similarly our neighbours on the lower side were shielded from view by our kitchen and outbuildings. No doubt my parents knew a little of the people in the adjoining houses, but for my part I was only aware that next below us lived a lady who had two little girls. Once or twice a smart young man in army officer uniform visited briefly; I hardly noticed him because so many young khaki clad figures, not to mention naval and airforce people came home for short leave from time to time.

Yet this was he who would give us an invaluable grounding in the practice and art of angling. Who told our neighbour that the two little lads next door wanted to fish I do not know, suffice it to say that he took us in hand, and recognising that there was no money for rods nor shops stocking them he taught us first to make our own. Three simple lessons have never been forgotten. First joining two hazel sticks, one lighter than the other, by cutting a long bevel end across the thicker end of the lighter stick, and matching it to another bevel end cut on the slimmer end of the heavier stick, so that when bound together the two formed a straight rod of sufficient length to be useful, while still capable of being taken apart for carrying or taking on a bus. Secondly he taught us how to coil tight turns of string round and round the two bevels, continuing until both cut ends were bound, and then the special finishing technique which left no string end dangling. Finally he showed how a short length of stout galvanised garden training wire, wound neatly round the shaft of a screwdriver would make a rod ring, two short ends turned at ninety degrees and flattened with a hammer such that the ring could be whipped to the rod.

He went back to the army, but we were about to start fishing. Once again we took our knives to the hazel bushes, looking carefully for two sticks that could be paired to make a good rod. This time we stripped off all the bark, and then started on the difficult task of cutting really flat bevels with a slightly weak knife. Out in the back yard with an old pair of pliers we cut our lengths of ring wire turning the pliers into wire cutters by the simple process of holding them against the stones and hitting them with a hammer. We were ready to go fishing, but would always find the task of whipping two rod sections together at the waterside too time-consuming, we wanted to get on with catching fish. So it was that my rod, once assembled, remained so unless I wanted to take it on a bus.

Fishing reels however were still in the future. At first we held little line winders with the rod, which sufficed for our purpose because our pond needed no long casting nor a reel for playing the fish, they were all tiny and each time the float dipped we could lift out another little roach.

The war was too close for comfort now, every week we heard bombs exploding a few miles away. The radio told of another great sea chase, as our navy pursued the battleship *Bismarck*, finally sinking it in mid Atlantic. It was a gripping story to rank with the earlier *Graf Spee* drama, perhaps given added publicity to deflect attention from the dreadful loss of our great battleship *Hood*, which had earlier been engaged with *Bismarck*, and had blown up following a direct hit in a magazine. Three of her complement of thirteen hundred men survived. The north African campaign left fewer dramatic memories in my young mind at that time, probably because our armies were in retreat.

In the middle of June I had a dream one night, the only dream I have ever remembered. I was standing inside my classroom window at school on a lovely fine summer day, looking out at the cricket match in progress on the square outside. As I watched a little red aeroplane approached, and started dropping red cricket balls. As each of these fell on the concrete drive beside the classroom it exploded with a loud bang. At that point mother came in and woke us up, asking if we were alright. We were, and so was she, but a stick of bombs had just fallen across Painswick demolishing the village centre, and as we later found out, destroying several other houses. In all eight bombs had been dropped, several within a few hundred yards of our house, but fortunately we suffered no harm and our home was undamaged. Many were less fortunate, and two properties on opposite sides of the village were bombed out in addition to the large group reduced to ruins in the Friday Street area. One or two bombs fell in open fields, the crater behind the line of chestnut trees in the field known as the Six Acres remaining, I remember, for several years.

This attack delayed our fishing plans, since our route would take us past two damaged areas where a lot of clearing up was going on. We had to lay our rods aside and take our amusement somewhere else. Avoiding the village, we followed a different lane down from home to the valley bottom. Beside the little stone bridge over the brook was a stile, indicating that a public footpath ran downstream from that point. Here then was an invitation to more exploration. This was a stream too big for paddling or wading, but interestingly various and with plenty of overhanging trees to provide concealment for birds. The only problem was that one often needed to cover the first few hundred yards downstream rather quickly to avoid the ever present smell of the sewage works beside the bridge.

    Here we saw kingfishers, dippers, woodpeckers and warblers in addition to birds we had met before. Moorhens in particular lived here in considerable numbers. Now they were hay making again, though slightly differently from when we had first watched. This farmer was still using horses, in fact he had two cart horses, one rather bigger than the other, but he had in addition acquired a tractor. The big green Fordson had spiked metal wheels on the back, and we watched as it hauled loads back to the farm far faster than the horses. We kept out of the way, but keenly observed what everybody was doing, with the result that in later years when we were allowed to help we had a good idea of what was needed.

    Soon after the village centre was cleared there came one of the big war fund raising efforts, War Weapons Week. All manner of events took place, parades, auctions, stall markets and the like. On the last Saturday of the week a number of stalls were set up almost opposite our house, between the church gates and Mr. Hopkins' cobbler's shop. Among the items on offer were a litter of kittens. We begged mother to buy one, and after much persuasion she did so.

Our back yard, enclosed by high walls on three sides had long been a favourite concert hall for the local cats. They must have found the magnificent resonance especially gratifying yowling the night away, even as some odd humans use the bath. During the darker evenings we would creep through the kitchen to the far door, then dash out hurling lumps of coke at the retreating visitors. Later, after bedtime, the procedure was to pour a chamber pot full of water out of our bedroom window. These measures had seemed sufficient thus far.

But other people had pets, and we wanted one, certainly not a dog because that would have to be walked and would frighten all the birds and rabbits we wanted to watch. That little basket of kittens had offered the ideal answer, endearing little things which would grow up well capable of looking after themselves in the country. Now at last we had got our cat, a little tabby scrap which settled down in its new home as soon as our initial overenthusiasm for stroking it had subsided.

Of course it had to have a name. My brother and I frequently argued vigorously over such important matters, but in this instance the answer arrived unchallenged and at once. Cats liked fish, therefore the kitten must be called Chips. Nobody was prepared to argue with such a neatly logical conclusion. So Chips it became, another mouth for mother to feed.

In fact, like other mothers she coped remarkably well on the very small rations which were unlikely to get bigger until the course of the war took a turn for the better. Our school lunchtime sandwiches which used to contain Shippham's excellent pastes were now filled with a rough and tasteless substitute from another maker. We looked forward to the occasional treat of a different type of filling such as Heinz sandwich spread. The week-end joint was tiny, but the butcher had some offals and sausages to help, and occasionally a flush of eggs would provide the chance to preserve some in a bucket of isinglass. Beef dripping was unrationed, but keenly sought, and I came to be very fond of it spread on hot toast with a sprinkling of salt and pepper. Mother made fruit cakes using a mixture of dripping and margarine, and they were excellent, though tending to dry out after a couple of days.

Chips appeared quite satisfied with her rations, happily consuming porridge scrapings with milk for breakfast, meat and vegetable left-overs with gravy at lunchtime, with bread and milk in the evening. Bread soon became stale, and the jug of milk would be sour next morning, so nobody grudged her supper. The horse-drawn float would be back before breakfast and our jugs would be replenished with real fresh milk, topped by a thick layer of Jersey cream.

As far as my brother and I were concerned, we could still find a few unrationed sweets to spend our two pence per week pocket money on. Mrs. Jones had big gobstoppers, fruit chews, liquorice bootlaces and sherbet dips on her counter, but following the bombs Ireland's newsagents with its wider range of confectionery was flattened.

Somehow we had become accustomed to uncomfortable clothes. Last year's school uniform was this year's play clothing, and growing made them far too tight. Now clothes too were to be rationed, but that would make little difference as money was tight too. Some items were still taken very seriously, shoes in particular. Daniel Neal in Cheltenham retained my parents' loyalty as they had in London, and now we all set out on the big green double decker bus for the long ride beyond the edge of the hills to that pretty town with its broad tree-lined main street and London style shops.

The journey to Stroud, daily during term time had long since become commonplace, but the prospect of a trip to Cheltenham was a real thrill, passing land and villages we hardly knew. The view from the upper deck of our bus was superb, over the top of the walls and hedges to the beautiful panorama beyond. That sunny August day the bus climbed steadily along the flank of the hill overlooking the top end of the Painswick valley. Pale stone farms and groups of cottages were set among pastures near the brook in the bottom, stooked corn fields further uphill. Sheepscombe village sheltered in a gully opposite, Cranham marked the top of the valley, and all was outlined along the hilltop by a wide band of beechwood. Here and there driveways led off to big houses hidden privately from the road, while uphill to our left the strangely irregular outline of Painswick beacon rose above its fringing pines.

It was a spectacular way to look at the countryside, and the bus schedule allowed forty minutes for the run to the terminus off Cheltenham Promenade. Progress was comfortably leisurely. That lovely valley scene was not the only view our journey offered, no sooner were we beyond the crest and driving down through the woods than a much broader aspect appeared to our left. As the trees rushed past we could see right down onto the Severn plain, a great drop over pasture and orchards, with a village in the distance, and the city of Gloucester beyond.

Then a yet more magnificent scene emerged. As we rounded a sharp right hand bend we found ourselves on a stretch of fine broad new road leading to a big left hand hairpin. Uphill to our right the beechwoods still stood, but to our left a great landslide had stripped the slope only a few months before we had come to live in Painswick. The result was a totally uninterrupted panoramic view of Gloucester, Cheltenham and all places between and beyond, to the distant tall jagged hills that father told us were the Malverns. Approaching the hairpin with the big old quarry behind it we were looking at Cheltenham, through the bend and we were looking back at Gloucester.

At the next corner it was the nearer view that held our

attention. This time we were peering at the land only a mile or so away to our left where stood a big, cleverly camouflaged factory. We were not supposed to know anything about it, but the buses that set off daily from outside our house taking men and women in the Cheltenham direction to work, well before our school bus arrived were going to the Gloster Aircraft factory at Brockworth. It was the better part of a year since our last Cheltenham visit, and now we noticed that something had changed. There was a black dotted line across the fields short of the factory, and it stretched all the way to our main road. Then it followed the roadside in the Cheltenham direction and we could see that it comprised a dense line of black metal constructions which looked like giant versions of the paraffin heaters mother used to prevent frozen pipes. Indeed they were, their function was to produce an immense smoke screen if enemy bombers approached.

Brockworth looked safe enough at the moment, though the anti-aircraft battery on the knoll short of the big crossroads was fully manned. No air attacks had reached our area for weeks, not since the Painswick bombing in fact, and the general feeling was that Hitler had had to send most of his aircraft to assist his drive against Russia.

Once again the countryside changed and with the Cotswold scarp now far to our right we were travelling through an area of orchards and small paddocks all the way to the outskirts of Cheltenham. Past the fine spacious grounds of the College we turned across the Promenade to the bus station and our shoes.

Despite that horrid swollen gland in my neck I felt at the start of the new school year that prospects were improving. I quite enjoyed school work, and now at last that other school had gone and we could adopt a normal timetable; with a half day on Thursday, and Saturday for clubs and matches. I had been elevated to the second form with most of my now familiar classmates and I looked forward to a year without lengthy absences. My enthusiasm must have got the better of me because in each of the class test lists through the year I emerged top of the form.

At home it was jam making time, an allowance of preserving sugar having become available, and we all set off to pick blackberries. Much of mother's shopping was weighed out into brown paper bags, and all these she carefully laid aside in a drawer for re-use. Some would now be filled with fruit. On our visit to our little pond we had spotted a fine bank of bushes, and although they were a mile and a half from home, that is where we now went, leaving the nearer fruit for the many others looking for a share. In consequence we really did find prime quality berries. But there was one considerable problem. If too many berries were put in one bag, the weight of those above would squash one berry at the bottom, and a soggy hole would promptly appear in the bag. By the time we had all returned home our hands and clothes were richly stained.

Mother never threw away a jam jar, so we had no problem in that direction, but we did need apples to help the jam to set. At the top of our garden was a big tree, a Newton Wonder which produced fruit that would keep until the following Easter. The crop was not yet ready to pick, but there were a proportion of blemished fruit which had started to ripen early. These we now collected and blackberry and apple jam seethed in the big iron pan. Cellophane discs topped the jam in the jars, then paper caps were tied tightly across the top. Victoria plums were also plentiful and they too were used to make a jam which I preferred to blackberry and apple.

In the shortening evenings our bows and arrows occupied us once again. They were now much improved for several reasons. First we had acquired proper clasp knives of the sort which has one stout blade, a marlin spike on the reverse, and a shackle to hang it from a belt clip. These enabled us to produce heavier and better made bows and arrows. Secondly the knowledge of how to finish a whipping, a skill which we had learned when making our fishing rods, meant that we could fit really good arrow flights, closing the split behind the flight tight enough to take a powerful bowstring. For good measure we cut the heads off some small nails and tapped the shafts, cut end first, into the core of the arrow stick point, the extra front weight improving performance.

This, however, would be our last season of bow and arrow play. We had taken to testing the performance of our bows by standing at a distance from each other and shooting the same arrow from one to the other; aiming of course to miss the other bowman. We soon found that an arrow coming directly towards you is invisible, or rather my brother did. I shouted a warning, but he did not know which way to dodge and the arrow buried its nasty little nail in his calf. Fed up with targets and not really able to kill rabbits or otherwise find good use for our bows I loosed an unaimed arrow into a big beech tree in the park, and to the astonishment of both of us it returned with a rook, shot through, on the end of it. But it was Chips that finally led us to abandon bows and arrows. Since her arrival the back yard social club had become much more noisy, sometimes there were violent fights taking place. It was time for a really accurate weapon, we must now graduate to catapults. So we did, and for the next six years would never go to the fields without one.

Except on our Thursday half day, school ended at four 4 o'clock, and we joined the crowd from the other three schools competing for a place on the homeward school buses. Once indoors we hung up our coats and satchels and sat by the fire to warm up. Childrens' Hour on the wireless was now followed by the news, and gradually, as I approached my eleventh birthday, I began to comprehend a little more of what this war meant. The fighting was still a long way away, in north Africa so far as our own forces were concerned, and the Germans were also engaged against Russia, too remote to arouse serious interest. We were beginning to hear talk of the Americans joining the war, but nobody seemed to know much about this, nor what it might mean for ourselves.

Shortages, especially of foodstuffs, were our most obvious indication of the results of war, and now even more items were being rationed. Occasionally some pictorial evidence, a magazine or newspaper photograph, would give us a glimpse of the reality of bombing at home or fighting abroad. In addition we were now taken to the cinema from time to time, when a film suitable for the young was being shown, and the programme always included a news bulletin showing war pictures which helped further to educate us about the horrors of the real world beyond our cosy horizon. That news film was always what I most wanted to see, Disney's happy little fantasies which had brought us to the cinema were poor stuff by comparison. Just once did the main film leave a lasting impression, the awful magic effects in *The Thief of Baghdad* left me waking in a cold sweat for weeks. Mother must have anticipated that it was just another nice film for children.

Obviously things were likely to get worse, therefore we must start to make an effective contribution to the food problem. We must learn to use our catapults to kill rabbits. Three points had to be mastered. First, the weapon must be sufficiently powerful, secondly the projectile must be delivered accurately, and third we must stalk to within killing range. As autumn once more gave way to winter there were few rabbits to be seen, what we really needed was practice against a plentiful prey. Rats were the ideal answer, and moreover we could keep ourselves warm at the same time.

When the dustmen called each week they tipped the contents of our galvanised bin into their lorry, and when it was full drove to the lower side of the village recreation ground and tipped the load. This had been their practice for a long time, and the result was very interesting. All those little plumes of sweet smoke from the chimneys of the village meant a high proportion of ashes for the dustmen, and some of this material was still burning when tipped. The result, as those who ventured onto the tip soon discovered, was a great area of underground fires from which sulphurous smoke emerged here and there. Had we thought about it we might have realised the danger of falling through the surface crust into the furnace beneath that had been burning there for years.

Inhabiting the lower edge of the dump, well fattened on the domestic waste so regularly fed to them, were a large colony of rats. They could be relied upon to be active at any time, thus providing good sport for anybody sufficiently hardened to the sulphur fumes to enjoy catapult practice in a really warm environment even in dead of winter. The cottagers below were only too keen to see an attempt made to reduce the toll of the raiders who stole their precious chickens' eggs.

We soon found that my catapult was sufficiently powerful. I had bought it in Stroud, and it had a flat wooden handle with gutta percha cords and a neat leather grip for the missile. Frequent practice on the tip soon taught accuracy, when spring arrived I could tackle the problem of the approach stalk.

But now, not long before Christmas a most extraordinary event occurred. The Japanese launched a surprise attack on the United States navy at their Pearl Harbour base. Suddenly we found that we were at war not only against Germany but against Japan as well, though we did not expect to be bombed from the other side of the world. Soon the news was full of defeats for our forces in the Far East, and of Japanese invasions of islands and mainland in the western Pacific.

Now at last, in January 1942, we knew that the Yanks were coming, even to our own district. In early spring a small advance group arrived to construct a radio communication and aircraft navigation facility on the high ground near Miserden, and they had to be billeted in private homes in the village. One of their number lodged with us for a few months. In the autumn of 1939 a small family from Birmingham had been billeted on us for a short time, and that had not been a very happy arrangement. Now, however, the arrival of Tex brought novelty and rejoicing as he dispensed things called candy bars, a form of confectionery previously unknown to us. He talked English, but in that strange way that one associated with films, and wore a very smart tailored uniform with badges and ranks quite unfamiliar to us. He was no trouble at all, off to work early in the morning and not back until evening, and he was most generous in sharing parcels of goodies sent to him by his family.

Unfortunately that little group had a lot of trouble getting to and from work, due to the narrow lanes and the style of their driving. They had several jeeps, tiny things with canvas tops and handles on the corners to assist in getting them back on their wheels, and a fifteen hundredweight lorry. They never seemed to work out a way of using one route to go to work and a different one to return home, with the result that all too often two of their vehicles, both going far too fast, met head on in one of our little sunken lanes, writing off vehicles and injuring their occupants. Tex survived but several of his team were casualties at different times. Theirs had been one of the essential preliminaries to the arrival of the American air force, and when the job was done Tex and his unit left us.

Just as their railway engines sounded so different from

ours, so the American aeroplanes sounded different too. Louder, harsher engine notes whether in large bombers or smaller fighter craft distinguished them from British machines; soon they would be a familiar sight and sound, though no American base was near us .

With the end of winter thoughts turned again to rabbits, and the need for catapult ammunition. Pebbles from the garden did not fly very straight, so we tried making our own lead shots. Drilling some shallow holes in an old piece of hardwood, we melted a bit of waste roofing lead in a cocoa tin lid on the gas stove, then lifting the lid with a pair of pliers we poured the molten lead into our drilled holes and left it to cool. The result was quite a good shot, but the process was both laborious and dangerous and we decided to abandon it.

Some of the pebbles in the garden however looked like tiny shellfish turned to stone, and indeed that was just what they were, fossils, the petrified remains of long extinct shellfish, These were smooth, and though not spherical flew remarkably straight from a catapult. There were a few scattered among the stony topsoil in our back garden, but in some of the local quarries we had found levels where many could be collected. In those quarries we found another interest, jackdaws nested in old rabbit holes and clefts in the rock, thus the arrival of young rabbits and the bird nesting season brought us to the same place for ammunition and jackdaws' eggs.

That Easter Saturday afternoon we were playing on Painswick beacon, and had gradually wandered all the way to the jackdaw quarry beneath the old fort itself. The weather was dull and cloudy but we could keep ourselves amused. The winter frosts had cracked plenty of little fossil shells out of the top face of the quarry, and they had rolled down the muddy slope to join the scree at the bottom. Soon we both had a couple of pocketfuls of catapult shot. There was no scope yet for collecting jackdaw eggs, the quarry face mud was far too slippery for us to approach the nesting holes near the top.

It was time to go home, but first we would climb the last few feet to the top of the beacon just to look at the view. The wind and cloud had drowned the sound of approaching German bombers. Just as we reached the summit we heard loud explosions in the vale below, and saw two black aircraft apparently bombing that camouflaged Gloster Aircraft factory at Brockworth. For a couple of minutes we watched, fascinated at our first sight of German raiders in action, but as soon as our anti-aircraft guns opened fire we found ourselves surrounded by the horrid whine of shrapnel shell splinters. We turned and sprinted off the bare hilltop for the cover of the pines, then continued running along the flank of the hill until we reached the top of the beech plantation. We had better cover there, but still we ran until at last we arrived, very blown, at our own front door. The anti-aircraft guns had been firing from far below us at low flying aircraft, with the result that we had been much too close for comfort to their line of fire. Later we heard that the raiders had continued to attack for nearly half an hour. Fortunately that was our closest encounter with the enemy.

Father, on the other hand, had been living and working in London during the heavy German bombing. Each day he caught the train to work, often delayed by bomb damage. In the evening he ate a quick meal and then spent the night on fire-watch duty. He had never been very strong, and after hundreds of nights on duty his health at last failed, and he resigned his post at St. James' club and came to live with us at Painswick. He found a tiny office in Stroud where he put up his brass plate as a Chartered Accountant. By now we boys were capable of keeping ourselves occupied in the countryside, which was just as well with our little home becoming that much more crowded.

A fine mid-June Saturday brought the end of the fishing close season and out came our hazel stick rods, line winders and end tackles and we set off once more down the steep slope of Tibbiwell lane. Last year's bomb damage had now been tidied and the spring water was running clear down its little gutter once again. Up the deep lane opposite to the hilltop, then down the ridge to join our old stone road to the valley bottom we went, wild flowers in profusion everywhere.

Our little pond was still there, the new season's sedges and reeds growing up around the sides, well trodden fresh cow muck on the old roadway across the end. Yellow dung flies swarmed over the muck, myriads of smaller flies circled over the pond. Our bait was a tiny ball of bread paste on the point of the hook, with a little goose quill float to indicate a bite. Ignore the flies, only some of them sting, but fix the eyes on that float.

In fact there were a very large number of fish in that pond, about the size of sardines, and they were not sufficiently educated to be hook shy. Quite soon the bit of old newspaper we had brought to wrap the catch had more than twenty little roach in it. Chips the cat was going to have a treat, and her needs were going to continue to give us every excuse to visit our pond.

Frequent bites were a much needed encouragement, for fishing soon became rather tiring; thanks to the cow muck there was nowhere to sit down. Without our knowing it the magic of the scene began to charm us, the rich green of the pastures, the paler shades of the young willow leaves waving in the breeze mimicking the flashing ripples on the pond. Across this quiet background the bobbing moorhen pushed its vee shaped wake beside the sedges, the big green and yellow dragonflies swooped here and there rattling their great wings, whilst their daintier relatives the blue damselflies sunned their delicate bodies among the reeds. Warblers and finches were busy in the alders, swallows nesting in the barn continually flashed past to scoop more flies off the water surface.

The quiet backdrop overlaid with such an enchanting variety of wildlife activity is the real lure of the angler's hobby, we scarcely recognised its influence then, but it has possessed us over all the long years since.

Father's move from London, coinciding with a lull in German air attack, enabled us to make a brief visit to our former home near Wimbledon during the school summer holiday. For one incident only I will never forget that trip. The wretched swollen gland in my neck still oozed a little, but the dressing had been removed to let the sunshine get to it. The next door neighbours had a couple of boys rather older than ourselves, and one afternoon we joined them in the old orchard behind their house to play cricket. This was not proper cricket of course, just four lads taking turns to bat and bowl. The trouble was that the bat and ball were indeed proper cricket kit, and I soon learned how hard the ball was when struck by a much larger boy. Having stung my fingers more than once I was in no mood to wait when the ball was hit straight at my face. I flung myself sideways and the rough bark of an old pear tree ripped the side of my neck open, swollen gland and all.

I was a terrible mess, and the doctor had to be summoned to tidy me up. The swelling the surgeons had left alone had been effectively gouged out by the tree, it remained only for the wound to be cleaned and the flaps of skin put back approximately in place before I was fixed up with an even bigger dressing than ever before. A sad memory for that last visit to the old home, and yet it was very important. At last the wound healed and I was pronounced fit to take part in gym lessons and cricket, though still barred from swimming and rugby.

Those benefits were still in the future, for the rest of the summer holiday I had a very sore neck and carefully avoided adventurous games. Nevertheless I was not prevented from walking my usual haunts and noticing the camp under construction in Painswick park. Another could be seen on the westward hill at Edge, with tanks roaring around the nearby common in clouds of dust.

The really important fact was that we now felt free to roam the countryside without worrying mother, though we still made sure she knew in what direction we were going, whether to the beacon, the stream, the pond or stalking rabbits on one farm or another. Where we were going was known, when we would return was not. Watches were inaccurate and easily broken, we relied entirely on guesswork where time was concerned, and always came home late. It had happened gradually, yet it was terribly important to us after so many years bound to apron strings, from now on we were independent.

# CHAPTER 6

It was now three years since our arrival from London, and within the limits of our school on the one hand and the valleys near our new home on the other, most things were now familiar. We no longer felt ourselves strangers cautiously exploring in an unknown land.

Along the way there had of course been some especially memorable highlights in our wanderings, as on that sunny summer day when we walked along the farm track to the point where the spring rising below Painswick House washed the stones white as it formed a little ford across our way. Looking into a few inches of water we saw for the first time those groups of tiny pebbles which moved about in the stream bed. Then we realised that there were some legs at one end of these strange structures, and on picking one up found a hollow cylinder in which lived a creature which not only had legs, but also a jolly good pair of jaws at the open end of that case. We had found caddis fly larvae.

Fascinated now by that clear shallow water we began quietly turning small stones to see what else lived in the ford. Soon we had met our first bullhead, and our first crayfish. Suddenly that tiny brook was not just another puddle to splash through, it had introduced us to its inhabitants whose existence we had not previously guessed.

There were other wonderful memories from bright sunny days, as when we crept into the damp derelict cottage at Dutchcombe and found owls' eggs in the chimney. On the edge of Catswood in a planting of young larch trees we had crawled beneath the branches and been rewarded with our first really good view of goldcrests.

From a grey cold autumn Saturday afternoon came

another unforgettable experience. Warmly clad in our school gaberdine raincoats and wellington boots we were moving quietly through the fields keeping our eyes open. Ahead the land started to fall away to a broad bank of brambles above the brook. Short of the bushes we could see an old tweed cap. We were about to meet Peter, though there would be no conversation. Under that cap sat a mackintoshed figure, still and silent, though something was moving in his left coat pocket. We knew he was ferreting and we must not make a sound. Quietly we walked up and sat down some yards away to watch. Suddenly, a little to his left a rabbit in a net shot out of a hole and he quickly grabbed it, killed it and replaced the net. The ferret took a look outside and then went back down the hole. It was cold and damp, dripping nose weather, and Peter obviously had a cold. As for the rabbits, they too must have been uncomfortable. It had been a very rainy autumn and their burrows would have been running spring water, that dead rabbit had emerged soaking wet. Peter placed a thumb against each nostril in turn and with a sharp blow of the nose discharged the contents of the other nostril. Then he picked up the rabbit and wiped his nose on it.

We left him sitting there, his line ferret still in its bag in his pocket, and retreated as quietly as we could until we were far enough distant to relieve our pent-up laughter.

So much for earlier memories, now we were becoming impatient, feeling a need to expand our horizons. We had found that many of our school friends also enjoyed fishing, and they lived in different parts of the five Stroud valleys to which we had no transport. Many of these boys had bicycles, and we now came to see the acquisition of our own cycles as a most urgent requirement in order to add variety of venue and company to our fishing. There was no money for bicycles, my two pence weekly pocket money could never produce savings sufficient to buy one, we could only hope for a change of fortune.

School life so far had been fairly relaxed, but now, at the start of a new school year I began to feel a certain seriousness. In four years time I would be one of those entered for examinations on which all future study depended. Four years was far ahead, but each September it would be one year closer. Homework became a little more difficult, but what would it be like, I wondered, when one joined the ranks of those senior boys I saw coming to school each morning with a great pile of books.

The war news too gave good cause for a serious attitude, and the sight of American troops around the district provided a constant reminder of the dreadful military catastrophe in the Pacific which had brought them. The long trains carrying angular British army lorries and tracked carriers were now loaded with the heavier and more rounded American vehicles. It was a little odd that the Americans called their railway trucks waggons and their lorries trucks, but they had not been here long enough to master English completely.

During the previous school term boys had started joining the army cadet corps, an excellent idea it seemed to me if I was going in future to go from school to the army as so many of our school-leavers were doing. At eleven years old I was too young, but it would be my aim to join as soon as possible.

Meanwhile with winter approaching and so many things in short supply, there was urgent need to gather fruit for jams, and to store the crop on our big apple tree. Our house had a large cellar, no longer used as a coal hole, and with the well head securely covered it became home for the big apple rack from our London home. This was really a big stack of shallow slatted drawers, where the apples, each carefully wrapped in a square of newspaper, kept cool until needed. So large was the crop that a local carpenter was asked to make another rack.

The general seriousness I had felt that autumn had many components, but especially I was aware of large numbers of our bombers flying south at night, road convoys which rumbled through the village almost unlit through the long hours of darkness, those trainloads of vehicles which passed the school almost daily. The news was still of defeat in the Pacific and retreat in the western desert, but at the same time it was obvious that something was about to happen.

In the last week of October news arrived that our army had broken out of its position at El Alamein, then a fortnight later we learned of allied landings far to the westward on the north African coast. As I approached my twelfth birthday it seemed to me that this war was going to go on for a very long time, and would involve me before it was over. With the aid of my school atlas it was obvious that if we were to beat the Germans and Italians we had to mount at least two seaborne invasions, and how that could be done was far beyond my comprehension.

Nevertheless things were changing. The quiet countryside was quiet no longer. Day and night the sound of aircraft was everywhere, the distant thunder of high flying bomber groups, the roar of passing fighters, the rumble of transport and trainer planes made aircraft recognition every boy's hobby. I remember listing over thirty types of British and American aircraft I had seen. German planes no longer troubled us, but every approaching sound or silhouette had to be checked just in case. In spite of so much reassuring air activity it therefore remained a very tense time.

The dark evenings soon returned, and we saw little of the American troops until the spring, preferring to spend our week-ends roaming the fields. But the evidence of their presence was everywhere, unfamiliar soft cigarette packets and chewing gum. We had only seen chewing gum in little fat packs of sugar coated cushion shaped pieces, now the Americans were unwrapping strips. Then too there were those little damp deflated balloons, some coloured, some knotted, which appeared in corners and gutters. What they were for we had no idea, but they had appeared since the coming of the Americans.

One or two advantages arose from the arrival of father. Among his first clients was farmer Herbert from Skinners Mill farm. This was that farm in the valley where we had watched the haymakers and found birds' nests along the brook. We had wandered freely without seeking permission to stray from the footpaths, but now Mr. Herbert told father that we boys were welcome on the farm provided that we did not cause trouble, and he and his wife would keep an eye on us.

Previously we had confined our activities to the waterside meadows downstream of the lane, on the upstream side stood the farm buildings and farm house, beside a very pretty mill pond, and these, with the fields beyond became a new area to explore. Over the years we came to know the farm well, but at first we were content to be able to shelter in the entrance to the long shed when rain threatened us with a soaking.

The long shed, as it was known, was in fact a stone built cowshed originally, standing between the farm drive and the Painswick brook. It had become a general store and garage and contained such a variety of tools and equipment that it would take us many visits to find them all or understand their purpose. The long earth floor made it an ideal place to park the tractor, fuel and oil leaks were promptly absorbed, leaving just the smell for which I will always remember that shed. The broad stone ledges along either side displayed hand tools and big spanners, and various things for attaching other equipment behind the tractor. Against the wall above hung the cart-horse harnesses and tackle, while toward the back of the shed stood two small carts. A bundle of mole traps hung from a nail on the wall, and on top of one of the great cross beams below the roof lay an old twelve bore shotgun. Just to shelter from a storm was an education as we tried to understand what various odd shaped articles were.

Father felt that we ought now to have a proper sledge, and the local builder's carpenter was asked to make one. Long and low, with broad steel-shod runners, the platform on top was unusual in that it was not formed from planks with parallel sides. In fact the seat was constructed from a number of pieces whose sides ran at angles to the front board. Having seen the effect of crashing one runner of a sledge against a gatepost at speed, whereupon a plank seated structure became twisted, we rightly assumed our sledge would prove much stronger. Indeed it was, but the feature we thought to be deliberate design had only arisen because the half inch elm platform was made from coffin lid off-cuts.

This great sledge, big enough to seat two to prevent squabbling, nearly defeated us at first. The sheer weight of the thing needed all our strength to drag it up the street and on up the hill to the beacon. We tried it out at first on a quite gentle slope, which was just as well. It was soon apparent that once this great weight took off it would require a lot of effort to steer or stop it. Nor could we just abandon ship lest the sledge run on and injure a bystander. It was quite a responsibility.

In an effort to maintain control we first tried to ride it in fresh snow and uncut grass. The conditions certainly slowed the sledge, but the loose snow piled up under our belted raincoats as we sat, and we were soon soaked from the waist down, and very cold. Now we could appreciate why more experienced boys rode face down and head first over the more hard packed runs. They were far less likely to get a wetting. It was a very discouraging start, next year we would be stronger and more confident I hoped.

That winter of 1943 was a gloomy time. Fuel was in short supply, and our coal fires were now burning logs. They did not last as long as coal, nor did they give as much heat, and the mouldy smell of the stacked wood in the cellar seemed to pervade the house. Each fresh load had to be carried right through to the back yard, where my brother and I would then spend hours with hammer and iron wedges splitting the logs to usable size.

Food rationing remained a problem for mother, and supplements were always welcome. Two ladies who walked a couple of miles each way carrying baskets of skinned wild rabbits each Saturday often found her happy to buy. They certainly made a very tasty meal.

Under the rationing rules a farmer could surrender his bacon ration coupons and be allowed to kill a pig of his own instead. By chance we came to know just what this involved. We had gone down to the farm, and noticed an unfamiliar van parked some way up the drive, beside a small stable. Outside stood several large metal bowls and a small pile of straw. Looking over the stable door we could see a block and tackle hanging from the centre beam, three men and one pig. A loop from the tackle was fixed round the pig's back legs.

The action was so fast that we were left gaping. Using something like a pistol to the animal's head the pig was stunned. Immediately two men on the rope hoisted the carcase by the hind legs to hang from the beam. Its throat was cut right across and blood gushed into two big bowls on the floor. Next the underside was cut open from beneath the tail to the ribs, and with one more nick a great mass of writhing grey tubes fell steaming into yet another bowl. Then the butcher's arm went right up inside the ribs, another cut and out came the rest of the vitals, lumps of different shapes, sizes and colours into yet another metal container.

Handfuls of straw were lighted to singe off all the animal's hair, and in a few minutes the job was done and the naked body minus its internal machinery was in the back of the van. We were told it would now be taken away to be cured. Surely they could not cure that pig after all they had done to it that morning, we realised that there was a second meaning to that word cure.

As we walked away a small group of cows lay quietly chewing the cud in the home paddock. Watching their jaws I remember thinking that if only one or two of them had been smoking cigars they would have more clearly reminded us of gum chewing American soldiers.

The return of spring again emphasised our need of bicycles. Our only chance of earning lay in working where we could for a few pennies per hour, and at that rate bicycles would still be years away. A very eminent local naturalist who had helped to answer some of our questions when we had found something beyond the scope of our reference books, let us come and help his old gardener tending the borders of his big garden. I presumed that other garden staff had gone to the war, the place could never have been maintained by one man.

Then we tried making coal dust briquettes. Official leaflets had pointed out that coal cellar sweepings combined with a little cement and left to dry in a small flower pot lined with newspaper would form a useful solid lump that would burn well. One of the cottages in the middle of the village had a coal cellar that had not been swept for years, and here we set about briquette making. The dust that rose in the confined space of that cellar filled noses, eyes, ears, hair and all our clothes. The small reward we brought home was certainly not worth mother's labour in cleaning us up. The fifteen shilling savings certificates we were given at Christmas each year did not amount to much when the cost of a bicycle was needed, and we could not cash them without parental approval. Desperately as we wanted to extend our range we really had no means of obtaining cycles.

Meanwhile we were growing to understand a little more about the war. While father was still in London he had brought glossy magazines home when he came down for the occasional weekend. The Sphere and the Illustrated London News contained pictures of important people and photographs of war scenes, but since he joined us at Painswick that supply had dried up. I presume these magazines were out of date copies from the club where father had worked, now he brought home the Picture Post each week from Stroud. This too showed pictures from the war and gradually we at last began to have some visual idea of what war entailed.

The news on the wireless was becoming more exciting as we heard of British and American success in driving the Germans out of north Africa, the Russians pushing them back too, while the Americans were fighting their way across the Pacific islands. Last year's gloom was lifting as the summer approached. Then suddenly we had a ghastly shock. With the arrival of American troops had come also Life magazine, similar to Picture Post but far less restrained. In one edition the entire front cover was devoted to a close-up picture of a mound of dead Japanese, appearing as if sprinkled with rice. In fact the rice was maggots. At last our young eyes told us the reality of war. Next time we saw a picture of a knocked-out tank we would be able to visualise something of its interior.

Our kind neighbour came home on leave, and managing to get a little petrol for his car took us fishing at Cherington. Far beyond our range until we could afford cycles it was a very beautiful place, the triangular lake bounded by tall beeches on the sides flanking the outflow sluice and dam, the third side grass rising to pasture fields beyond a little lane. Close to the dam stood a very big boathouse, its timber structure painted bottle green, its upper floor giving onto a broad balcony with white painted balustrade, the whole building overhung by the branches of an enormous weeping beech.

Standing on that balcony looking down into the clear water it was obvious that this was quite a deep lake. Sedges and reeds around the edge, then a broad fringe of water-lilies, beyond patches of bright green water weed showed beneath the surface. Coots and moorhens were foraging among the lilies, while farther out swam mallard and the constantly disappearing dabchicks. I was not surprised to hear that there were big carp out there, but we were hoping to catch some of the perch for which the lake was noted. Fishing from the balcony was a risky business, the overhanging beech waiting to snatch the tackle whether on cast or retrieve, and we soon realised that the bank along the dam sloped so steeply to deep water that this was the best place from which to fish. We had no great bag that day, but the picture of that enchanting lake remained with us adding further to the imperative itch for bicycles.

The annual war savings drive returned in the summer, with a variety of events including parades, auctions and sales of craftwork and unwanted possessions. This year Wings for Victory Week brought out the trestle tables again, opposite the Town Hall. Among the assortment of goods on offer one item especially caught my eye. Against the end of one table was propped an old ladies' bicycle. At first I thought it belonged to somebody running the stall, then I had a closer look and saw a price label £3 on it.

It was far from ideal, I was not yet thirteen and that full size bicycle was too big for me. However, it had no crossbar and if the saddle and handlebars were lowered I was sure I could master it. Mother needed a lot of persuading, but in the end father found three pounds for a good cause and my brother and I had a bicycle to share.

We had learned to cycle on the beach in France five years earlier, now we had to start all over again. Our new bicycle had only one gear and to start it moving we needed a stretch of level road. Crossing the beacon between the Gloucester and Cheltenham roads, passing the cemetery and the golf club was an ideal length. We had to push our machine up to the start of the beacon slopes, but then we could take turns riding to the golf club and back. Quite soon we could manage without falling off, and we felt this was a very important step towards having proper cycles although the limitations were obvious. Only one of us could ride the bike at a time, and with only one gear it was of no real use in our hilly countryside. We just had to accept that a quick dash down the valley must be followed by a hard push walking up the other side.

We had only thought of bicycles as a way of getting to the various fishing lakes in the Stroud valleys, now we were going to learn another use, the cycle as a toy. A number of the village boys had bicycles, single speed for the most part. They had no ambitions to ride long distances but had great fun riding up and down the grassy mounded areas of the beacon. Soon we were joining them, making contact once again with lads from the upper part of the village, because lately our favourite play areas had been down the hill on the valley farms. We quickly learned the problems of riding on the beacon, and had to find the price of tyre levers and puncture patches provided by Mr. Musgrove.

Before the war Mr. Musgrove had sold bicycles, and even now sometimes had a few new ones. A visit to his shop fuelled our burning ambition to have our own new three speed cycles. That ambition would have to continue smouldering for a long time yet.

Finding our amusement on the hill rather than around the farm, we saw a lot more of the American troops. A hutted camp had been built for them in Painswick park and we were very impressed by their smart appearance. We did not realise that we were seeing them in what they called their walking out dress, and automatically compared it to the heavy serge battledress of the British soldier. They wore their forage caps straight rather than sloped to the right in the British fashion, and their smooth tailored tunics and trousers looked very smart, though rather too tight across the seat. Those trousers were not made for bending to play skittles, though probably free enough for darts.

My brother and I had had no contact with them so far, and we now found out that some of our friends had been into the camp in the evenings after school and joined in baseball games, a form of rounders with the ball travelling at such a speed that players caught it with big padded gloves.

During school lunch hours and morning breaks much of our interest in fine weather lay in throwing balls. Cricket demanded the ability to throw fast and flat over the stumps, and most of us had become fairly proficient at this round-arm return. In consequence our American friends found us well able to adapt to baseball, at least so far as throwing, catching, and even pitching were concerned. The bat swung horizontally rather than held in the vertical was far more difficult to master, but not all the Americans were good strikers.

We rather shyly tagged on to the group visiting the camp after school, and like our friends were very warmly welcomed, seldom returning home without a bar of candy. There were many brands and types of this confectionery, completely different as it seemed to me from British bars. All we had seen apart from plain or filled bars of chocolate squares were Mars and Milky Way. American candy contained all manner of ingredients, some crunchy, some sticky, and all very sweet.

As usual we were aware of long trains loaded with tanks and army lorries passing the school, road convoys rumbling past our home all through the short summer night, and more and more continuous air activity. The war was ever with us, however distant the fighting, and now came news that the allied forces had invaded Sicily. I looked again at my school atlas and could see how we must drive the Germans up from the bottom of Italy. It was a time of mounting excitement.

Just before the end of summer term we found to our great surprise that the long wood beside the Gloucester road, opposite Painswick park was full of black American soldiers. I had hardly ever seen a black man, and now here they were in hundreds, all shapes and sizes, living in little two man bivouac tents each surrounded by a shallow hexagonal scrape to drain rainwater. One of their favourite pastimes was a game similar to deck quoits, but played with big iron horseshoes. A short stake was pushed into the ground, and from a set distance the shoes were thrown, quoit fashion with the object of ringing the stake. Those horseshoes gradually gouged out a dusty pit around the stake which remained visible for years afterwards.

Over on the reclaimed tip ground toward the cemetery, the only level piece of land nearby, they laid out a small version of a baseball pitch, and we were introduced to softball. This employs baseball kit with a large ball far softer than a baseball, with the result that it can be played in a fairly limited area.

These black soldiers were delighted to welcome our inquisitive bunch, and soon involved us in softball. One exceptionally tall man, Tiny of course, made it his job to show us the ropes. We soon made a very important discovery, the black troops ate their evening meal at six o'clock, the whites in the park at seven. An interesting routine emerged.

Home from school we dashed up the hill to play softball

with the black soldiers, who then gave us mess tins and lined us up with them at their field kitchen. Afterwards it was possible to cross the road and repeat the process with the white Americans, though we seldom had room for much more food. After their meal some who knew the game stayed to play chess. These white Americans seemed puzzled that we should visit the black troops, who we always saw wearing overalls rather than the whites' smart uniform.

From that contact with men living in field conditions we again expanded our knowledge of the demands of warfare, no solid roofs, no running hot water, no flush lavatories.

Those black Americans used a lavatory of extreme simplicity. A trench some three feet wide and two feet deep ran straight for about twelve feet. The excavated soil and stones were heaped along the sides, and a four foot high screen of hessian was erected right round the area a yard or so from the trench, its ends overlapping to improve privacy, but sufficiently far apart to leave an entry corridor. At each end the trench was spanned by two large logs in the form of an inverted vee, their ends overlapped and lashed. To these supports two long logs were then fixed, running the length of the trench, about three feet above ground level and leaving about a foot between the logs. This was a lavatory seat capable of accommodating the needs of a number of people at once. Another pair of long logs were similarly fixed on each side about half way to ground level as a footrest.

That long wood beside the Gloucester road was a favourite play area for us, but now as a military camp it was out of bounds. This really did not matter because the soldiers came out over the low stone boundary wall onto the hillside to play horseshoes or softball and their presence was novelty enough to compensate. Moreover the slope of the hill gave a clear view over their hessian screen and we could often see an assortment of black bottoms, or seated figures, elbows on knees, some reading a book, others smoking a cigar. It seemed a private rather than a sociable business, but we were very impressed with the simplicity of this structure which we were told was a crow-perch.

I could only think of one objection, users needed to be sure they had left no coin or valuables in hip pockets before lowering their trousers.

Then suddenly the wood was ours again, all those black soldiers had left in the night. There was little to show that they had ever been there, except for the FOUL GROUND notices at each end of the trench, now filled in, that had served their crow-perch. It was all very exciting, the war news was getting better and some day it was obvious that the allies would invade France. Meanwhile we could think about the things we saw, but not talk about them. The slogan CARELESS TALK COSTS LIVES had been drummed into us from placards and newspaper advertisements for years; but it seemed obvious that those missing soldiers had moved nearer to the enemy.

Then came a good example of how the war could complicate an ordinary domestic matter. Father received a telegram reporting the death of his old uncle who lived in the Isle of Man. As his sole executor some means had to be found of getting there. No ferry was available and father found himself taking a ride with the RAF in an aircraft not built for passenger carrying. A noisy and very uncomfortable business we were told, but at least the old man was given a decent burial and his affairs put in order.

Although the war scene seemed to be improving the problems of food rationing were as difficult as ever, making the occasional extras reaching the shops especially welcome. One product had been sent from Australia, tinned pork meat. This chopped pork had a wonderful smell unlike any other brand we had met, and the top and bottom of the tin were well packed with lard. Carefully scraping off this fat, mother would make the pastry for a pie, and then stretched the chopped up pork meat by mixing in breadcrumbs, chopped onion, a bit of cold cooked potato and a pinch of herbs. The result was one of the most memorable meals of our war, and a very rare event.

Back to school for the start of the autumn term and excitement grew as we heard of the surrender of Italy, though we soon realised that all the German troops there would fight on.

This was no time to concentrate on school work, the distractions were so many and varied. In the school lunch hour I watched as some of the senior boys in their khaki battledress and black boots practised rifle drill with wooden guns, that was where I wanted to be as soon as I was old enough. Among the many aeroplanes filling the skies we now had one without propellers, very fast and very noisy, how it flew was beyond me.

Strangest of all were towed gliders, flimsy looking affairs presumably intended for carrying troops, they seemed to offer precious little protection against the bullet fired from below. The thought left me feeling most uncomfortable.

At home the bicycle had enabled us to take part in a favourite pastime of the local lads, following the fire engine. Burdock & Sons builders yard opened onto the narrowest part of the main street, and there lived the fire engine, crewed for the most part by Burdock employees. When called out to a fire the various tradesmen, working in different places around the village would come running back to the yard. Meanwhile the village lads were leaping onto their bicycles and assembling as quickly as possible in the street.

If the emerging fire engine turned right, up the hill, that was the end of the matter so far as the cyclists were concerned, but if it turned down the hill a furious pursuit game began. How no lad was killed I do not know, for we rode in a great mass of cycles, following as close as possible to the little red fire engine, with complete disregard for the fact that our brakes could not match those of the vehicle we were following. It was all wonderfully exhilarating, and a rare treat since fires did not all occur in school holidays or after the bus had brought us home.

Once again the dark evenings returned, and again the tomcats in concert in the back yard provided sport, this time for our catapults. But despite our best efforts Chips the cat kept on producing handfuls of tiny kittens for some reason or other. Chips had grown up and was no longer the little kitten we wanted to stroke, she was just something else that shared the home, and kept comfortable curled up in her warm basket when not out with her friends. As for the kittens they never lived more than a week, then mother popped then in a full bucket of water with a lid on top weighted by a brick, later burying then in the garden while we were at school.

We found another interest to occupy us on winter Saturday afternoons. Since our brief encounter with Peter we had had no further experience of ferreting, now we met Mr. Parks. We found him one day on one of Webb's grounds, sitting quietly in his mackintosh, his brown painted wooden ferret box beside him. Keeping silent we were able to see how to set a purse-net properly, how to handle a ferret, and how to kill a rabbit. We quickly realised that it was often possible to hear the rabbits running around beneath where we sat before one shot out into a net. We must have managed not to spoil his sport, for we soon found this quiet man willing to call for us on his way down the street and let us accompany him on his Saturday afternoon expeditions. Some time later I heard that he had to go ferreting because of a stomach condition that made him unable to eat red meat. On his more successful days mother would have one of his rabbits and produce a tasty stew.

Once again a wartime blacked-out Christmas was approaching, and I wondered how many more we would have in similar conditions before the war was won. In Italy fierce fighting still continued, the surrender of the Italians had not brought the rapid conclusion I had hoped for.

# CHAPTER 7

The doctors had at last relented and I was allowed to join gym classes at school. In a way it was very encouraging to be free of the unsocial isolation of those excused from taking part, who stood uncomfortably in the narrow space behind the wall-bars during the lesson. I enjoyed gym, and being very lightly built soon became a fairly competent performer, especially at agility routines.

But once again there was this awful business of having to take all ones clothes off in public, and after the class having to rush naked through the hot shower tunnel with the rest of the class before towelling quickly down and going to the next lesson. In winter getting changed into our cotton shorts made gym a very chilly experience, though the teacher soon had us moving sufficiently to warm up a little.

In one sense I was fortunate, the school canteen was now operating and a hot mid-day meal helped to restore me after so much unaccustomed exposure. Even after four years of war I was a rather choosy eater, but once a week bread pudding was served, so excellent that it remains my favourite memory of those meals.

As 1944 arrived there came a time when repeated snowfalls packed down by the wheels of lorries completely covered the little grit that had been spread to improve grip. Instead of dragging our big heavy sledge up onto the hill, it now seemed possible to ride it down the main Stroud road. The surface being tightly compacted it was difficult to prevent the sledge sliding sideways on corners, but a number of us enjoyed the thrilling experience of lying on our sledges outside Painswick churchyard, gliding slowly round the lych-gate corner, then gathering speed rapidly approaching the right and left turns at Lullingworth corner.

Those who hit the kerb here inevitably overturned into the hedge but many of us succeeded in riding on at a good speed all the way to the bottom of the hill at the Washbrook. As it happened the opportunity to attempt that sledge ride never returned, which is sad because it was a thrilling experience.

Through those dark winter months the war news was very frustrating. The wireless told of great allied bombing raids on Germany, of the Americans beginning to regain ground in the Pacific, and of the Russians raising the siege of Leningrad. But in Italy we were having a very difficult time. I presumed that even there winter weather was making the job more difficult.

That was only one side of the story of course. We still heard the convoys rumbling through the night, not just lorries but guns as well, always going south. If that sort of thing was happening all around the country then the invasion of France must soon follow.

The light evenings returned, the old bicycle was brought out again, and we tramped up the beacon to ride it up and down the mounds with the other lads. One bright, cool morning in May several of us had pushed our cycles up as far as the top of the long wood, moving quietly as we always did, when we all suddenly stopped. An unmistakable smell had reached us on the breeze. Only a faint whiff, but there was no doubt about it, somebody nearby was frying some of that wonderful Australian pork meat.

Silently we lowered our cycles and crawled to the edge of the old Victoria quarry, its deep gully long since abandoned, was flanked with pebble scree growing small pine trees. We knew the place well, it was a favourite spot for our stalking games. There in the bottom of the gully was an oblong brown tent.

A few yards away a man in khaki battledress was carefully turning the contents of a frying pan over a small camp cooker.

We crept away leftward through the broken ground until we were well below the tent, and saw the small canvas covered lorry hidden among the trees. We walked on towards the tent.

"Hello lads, just the people I wanted to see" called the cook, who we could now see was in fact a British staff sergeant. He had raised his voice just a little louder than necessary to be heard by us, and now we noticed other people moving in the tent. Soon a sergeant, two more WO2s and a major emerged. They asked us where the nearest water supply could be found, and we told them to try Hill Farm. In our innocence we gave them just what they had asked, the nearest supply to where they were; if only we had better understood their business we would have directed then to half a dozen other places on both sides of the beacon.

However they seemed well pleased with our help, and we all enjoyed a great doorstep sandwich enfolding a slice of fried pork meat. It was absolutely delicious. We left without working out what these men were doing in Victoria quarry, we just assumed it was one more of those things you were not supposed to talk about. That evening the tent had gone.

A few days later we heard that the beacon was swarming with British troops, and we soon found that report to be correct. Among all the pine trees on both flanks of the hill camouflaged lorries stood beneath the branches, and hundreds of soldiers in red berets had dug themselves two man trenches. That must have been a terrible job on the very stony ground with only their trenching tools to help. I imagined that their little spike bayonets must have been used to break up the packed stones. It was an extraordinary sight, I have no idea how many hundreds of men were there, but now it became obvious that our friends in the brown tent were a reconnaissance party, the fact that they were only emerging from their tent for breakfast at half past ten in the morning probably explained by their having driven through the night to the beacon.

All over the hill everything seemed very well organised, obviously they had found ample water supplies. All these troops had arrived in the night, and a couple of days later they were gone. We felt that news of the invasion of France must come at any moment.

Meanwhile there was urgent work to do. The soldiers had not filled in their slit trenches, So we must conduct a thorough search to find what had fallen out of their pockets, or otherwise been left behind. It was a disappointing business. They had done a very good job of tidying up, but the puzzle remained, where had they dumped all their discarded rubbish? Looking down into Catbrain quarry we found the answer, the old lime kiln was full of loot.

Climbing up we found half full five pound tins of jam, cans of orange concentrate jelly, part tins of that marvellous pork meat, packs of twenty four hour rations, sweetened condensed milk, chocolate cubes; all manner of wonderful things to share out and take home.

At last the war news from Italy was getting better, and now we heard that the allied armies had captured Rome. That evening I was standing at the junction of Gloucester Street and Pullens Road talking to my friends when suddenly we heard aeroplanes, and from over the wood to the north came DC3s towing gliders, hundreds and hundreds of them as it seemed. We had seen gliders before but not in these numbers, nor as darkness approached.

The laboured rumble of the engines left no doubt, these aircraft and gliders were fully loaded, some time later that night they would be over France.

The war was a very terrible business, but somehow I had never had to consider it so intensely before. Up there were hundreds of men, packed tight together, many of whom would probably be dead in the next few hours. My young mind played over the different deaths I could imagine, without any background experience whatever on which to base my thoughts. Standing there looking up at all those aircraft I began to feel utterly horrified.

Of course we still did not know with certainty that the invasion would start that night, and I went home thinking more about what I had to do at school the next day, than about the war. As it happened our guess had been right, and by morning break on that Tuesday official announcements on the wireless had reached the school and all of us, juniors and seniors alike felt a wave of excitement which left us almost unteachable for the rest of the day.

The excitement soon passed, the question we had all been asking for months was at last answered, the invasion had started. Now we knew where all the aircraft formations, all the convoys of lorries were going, now a schoolboy could return to his normal summer interests. The opening of the fishing season was only a week away.

The laborious task of whipping two sections of fishing rod together had brought us to the stage where we would be happy to spend our few available savings on proper rods, and if possible reels as well. Taking the bus to Gloucester my brother and I found a tackle shop in Worcester Street which had some second hand items in stock. A ten foot greenheart trout fly rod caught my eye, it had an additional spare top section. I certainly was not going to be fishing for trout, but it seemed to me a useful looking rod. I parted with three pounds ten shillings, plus another ten shillings for a tiny old reel. I had chosen well, that rod served me for many years of coarse fishing, and has indeed taken trout when much later the opportunity arose.

My brother meanwhile had selected a Spanish reed bottom rod which proved equally useful. We began to have ambitions beyond the back pond at Steanbridge. A little further down the same brook, past the old farm and the big house was a long lake. At one time it had extended to the lawn in front of the house, now the upper part was silted up. The lower half of the lake was very easy to fish, with an unobstructed bank on both sides of a long narrow triangle of water. Our kind neighbour had a word with the owner, and thereafter we simply had to telephone doctor Horton and we would be told to call at the house, where we were given a neat handwritten permit to fish on that day.

We had little success there, the summer weed growth left few gaps for fishing, but we soon saw the many pike sunning themselves and made a note to return in winter once we had graduated to owning pike tackle. Our neighbour also introduced us to the owner of another lake which had the advantage of lying within reach of our bus route. The colonel's wife at Southfield House let us fish her lake, and allowed some of our friends who lived nearby to come too.

The house stood on one side of a little lane, on the other was a tall stone wall with a door in the middle. Beyond lay a long oblong vegetable and fruit garden bounded by high walls with trained fruit trees, the beds outlined by box hedges.

Through the gate in the corner of the far wall steps led up to the dam end of the lake. It was an ideal fishing position in that there were no obstructions behind to snag the tackle when casting. Apart from a few small clumps of reed the lakeside too was clear. The water unfortunately was not. A number of Aylesbury ducks swam and fed here, the consequence being very murky water. It became nevertheless a favourite place because the fish in that lake were perch.

Our earlier experience catching roach involved a fish with a small soft mouth which would often suck at a tiny knob of bread paste for a long time, scarcely moving the float. This could be a frustrating business, and the eventual disappearance of the float offered no clue to the size of the fish. Perch on the other hand had large hard mouths, and grabbed the bait decisively. Without any warning the float would disappear, and with it the bait unless it was constantly watched and the rod tip smartly raised as the float dipped.

Perch would not eat bread, but they could always be relied upon to take a small red active worm. These could not be found digging the garden, which only yielded big grey lob worms or little pale hard things with yellow tails. Now we had to explore cowpats and manure heaps. Fresh cowpats were no good, nor were old dry ones with the grass growing through them. But turn one a fortnight or so old and beneath would be several little red worms thrashing about on the ground. We gathered them into a cocoa tin filled with moss and in a few days they were ready for use. Straight from the ground they would have broken when hooked, that time spent wriggling through the moss toughened them. Scraping carefully around the edge of an old manure heap we found another type of worm, red body segments alternating with yellow ones looked as if they would attract fish, and indeed they did.

We had gathered a few of these worms once before when we were introduced to Cherington, but now we wanted to get a good supply to enable us to fish Southfield lake whenever the opportunity offered. Not only was it easy to get to, it was also our first chance to fish with our school friends. It was necessary to turn our cocoa tin over every day or two to avoid a lazy lump of worms accumulating in the bottom, and we had to be careful to keep it in a cool place out of the sun.

The perch bit boldly and fought hard, most of them about six ounces in weight, beautiful looking fish with dark stripes across the body, a dangerously spiked dorsal fin, and another sharp spike at the back of the hard gill cover. We soon learned to handle them carefully. I did not care to try eating something from such muddy water, but the cat was duly grateful once mother had cooked the fish and removed the head, fins and hard skin.

Yet again the war meant that we could not go away for a summer holiday, but frequent visits to Southfield lake filled our August days happily enough that year. But as the month advanced my thoughts turned more and more towards the next school term.

This time I would be in the fourth form, the last year before embarking on the terribly serious fifth, at the end of which one had to sit the School Certificate examination. Unless certain grades were obtained in that exam further progress in academic study was effectively blocked. I was no slacker at school, but now I must try to cope with the fact that all the work was going to get harder, the homework hours longer, and questions about that fourth year work might appear in the fifth year examinations. Whatever happened in the war, I was going to have a long hard winter.

Our war seemed to be making slow progress, the others in Russia and the Pacific could not hold our attention, now that at last we felt we had a war of our own in France. The Germans had started launching flying bombs against London, pilotless jet propelled aircraft which dived down and exploded when the engine cut out. Sadly one landed in the garden of our old home, I had never really wanted to return there, but now at last it was obvious to me that my future would remain in the Stroud valleys.

Before the end of August Paris had been liberated, but the Germans still appeared to have places from which to launch plenty of their flying bombs. I felt sure that one day I would be called up like those seniors leaving the sixth form, and I was determined to join the school cadet force as soon as possible where the knowledge of fieldcraft I had gained on the hills would be useful, and where I would be taught to shoot. Rather too young I joined the cadets and became one of those who arrived at school twice a week in ill-fitting khaki battledress rather than school uniform.

After school we paraded and learned basic drill using wooden imitation rifles. They were not very realistic but had the advantage of being light in weight. I was glad to learn to slope and present using a wooden rifle, proper weapons would be much heavier. When rifles at last arrived they were not only heavy but extremely long, ancient Ross rifles from some war long ago.

The week-ends brought the real fun, when we would take to the hills and woods to stalk and attack some other school's cadets with the officers acting as umpires. On some Saturdays we went to one of the local small bore rifle ranges, either at the drill hall in Stroud or at Ebley. Here we were taught how to handle rifles and live ammunition, though only .22 calibre. At Ebley the guns were American Mossburgs, short, light and not very good for target shooting. At the drill hall we used BSA target rifles which were heavier and longer in the barrel. With these I was pleased to find that I could produce quite good scores.

Having been taught proper shooting range discipline I found that I could be allowed to fire at the Painswick club. The skittle alley between the Institute hall and the bowling green was also used as a .22 rifle range, and now some of the senior members helped the younger generation to improve their scores. I came to know some of those people who owned rifles, and a year or two later they knew me well enough to allow me to borrow an air rifle occasionally.

This then became a very different autumn with all my interests centred on rifle shooting and the army cadet force. Homework left little spare time, all the news was still of war, and the Germans seemed to be putting up a hard fight. Then just before the Christmas school holiday I at last bought a proper bicycle. It came from the Hercules factory with a single gear, but Mr. Musgrove had a Sturmey Archer three speed gear axle in stock and built it into the wheel for me. Now at last I could fish those waters my school friends described so temptingly, and explore the district.

I made a very bad start. Having ridden this magnificent new machine over the familiar mounds of the beacon, I rode down the path from Catbrain quarry to the golf club, along a narrow track cutting across the steep side of the hill between the pine trees. The pine needles brought disaster. I started to skid on them, the bicycle turned sideways down the steep slope, and I fell off just before it crashed into a tree completely breaking the front wheel and forks. I had a very miserable walk home. Fortunately Mr. Musgrove managed to repair my now not so new machine.

That was the end of cycling over the hill so far as I was concerned. My transport was far too precious to allow any more stupid risks.

As Christmas approached everybody was wondering whether it would be the last to suffer the black-out; if only we could win the war quickly then the shutters would be discarded, street lights switched on, and all the living room lights glow in the winter darkness as I had never seen them in five winters.

All the time we had lived opposite that parish church which so handsomely dominates the village of Painswick no winter evening services had been held, and the same restraint had applied to all the different brands of Christianity for which the village provided. Baptist, Methodist, Congregational, Catholic, Quakers and Brethren all had their places of worship, the parish church being the only one that catered for two distinct brands under one roof.

We had been taken to church once a month or so, and each time we joined a number of others who waited outside the door until the hymn singing had died down. After a pause the door opened and another crowd of people emerged. We stood quietly aside as they walked away, all of them looking straight ahead, noses a little raised as it seemed to me. Then we in our turn went into church for a service of matins with sermon which was provided in addition to the sung communion which had just taken place. Those high church folk certainly seemed a loftier race than we Protestants, but what was good enough for the king was good enough for us.

In any case I could not have gone to the sung communion because I was not confirmed. That was soon to be put right. The new vicar had called on mother and she had agreed that it was about time for me to be presented to the bishop. Now I had to cross that churchyard in darkness each week to join the little group of candidates assembled in the vestry at the bottom of the church tower. It was just possible to follow the light coloured path without a torch, but I kept a little one in my pocket in case of accidents. For half an hour or so we were instructed in the spiritual aspects of our religion, and in the structure and significance of the communion service. Living so close to the hard facts of everyday life the spiritual aspect was beyond my grasp, though I certainly believed in God, without any real knowledge of divine intervention in my own life.

A fortnight before Easter 1945 the bishop came and confirmed us, thus giving me an alternative approach to Sunday. Without having to join the holy people at the 10 o'clock service I could go to the 8 o'clock said communion on the first Sunday of the month. The advantage of this was that my parents did not expect me to go to the 11.15 matins service as well, and I therefore had the rest of the morning after church to do as I wanted. The disadvantage lay in a couple of slim books. In order to be properly prepared to receive communion the following morning I was supposed to spend the whole of Saturday evening reading these spiritual preparation books, praying.

I often wondered how all those people who went to the sung communion service spent their Saturday evenings. I myself never really felt I had properly prepared, but I still went at 8 o'clock hoping for the best, especially if Sunday dawned fine.

At school there had been an important change. The headmaster had retired at Christmas. I had always been the sort of boy to avoid attracting his attention if at all possible. For the most part I had succeeded. The rather short figure, dark suited and gowned of Mr. Carter had always impressed by his quiet authority.

The new head, we had been told was to be a Mr. Eagles, from a school at Sedbergh. Father explained that Sedbergh was a tough public school in the frozen north. Climbing the steps to the platform for the first assembly of the spring term he could hardly have presented a greater contrast to the previous head. Tall and lean with jutting square jaw, black bushy eyebrows and toothbrush moustache he appeared to me a very daunting figure. His entrance was announced by much banging and creaking as he went, and we realised at once that he had an artificial leg. I remember thinking that if he proved to be somebody I would prefer to avoid, at least I would hear him coming.

Our war was much quieter now, the campaign still continued in Germany, and was always hard fought according to the wireless news broadcasts, but the great road convoys and bomber flights no longer passed. The threat of German air raids in our area was now much reduced, but safety must not be taken for granted. Over London and the east coast flying bombs still attacked, and another German secret weapon, a huge bomb delivered by rocket made me glad that we had left London. Much of our interest looking skyward on the sound of an approaching aircraft was now to see whether it was a Gloster Meteor, the twin engined jet propelled plane which had been developed from that first single engined machine with no propeller we had seen in earlier years.

Past Easter the war in Germany continued, but we began to realise that the battle must soon be won as less and less of their country remained in German control. At the end of the first week of May it was all over. The following Tuesday, 8th May was to be celebrated as Victory in Europe Day, VE day.

Now at last I had a job to do, together with all the other village lads. There was a beacon fire to be built. I joined a group hauling fallen beech branches from the strip of woodland beside the Gloucester road beneath the top of Painswick beacon, right up the steepest route to the edge of the ancient fortification where a huge pile of timber was gradually assembled. Other groups working among the pines on the east side of the hill were bringing in great quantities of material, and it soon became obvious that because the beacon top was so narrow the fire pile would have to be built with a tunnel running to the centre for it to be lit. One farmer's son drove a tractor round neighbouring farms collecting from each a gallon of tractor fuel and a gallon of waste oil. Others tried to think of a safe way of lighting our huge pile. One Painswick resident had been a keen amateur photographer before the war, and looking for something to make a fuse to light the fire from a distance we asked him if he still had any magnesium powder or ribbon. He gave us all his stock, but unfortunately it was old and too oxidised to burn properly. Over a couple of days the completely uncoordinated efforts of many groups of excited people produced an enormous heap.

Tuesday May 8th, and with high summer approaching it

was not dark enough to light the fire until nearly half past nine. The weather was perfect, and as our great beacon ignited we felt it must be visible for miles. As the evening grew darker the unrelieved darkness of so many wartime nights was finally and dramatically dispelled as dozens of other bright blazes lit up all the hilltops along our side of the Severn plain from Nibley to Cleeve, all the high ground of the Forest of Dean, the long line of the Malverns, with Bredon, Chosen Hill and Robinswood.

Below the distant hilltops still more fires could be seen, and as we looked down from the beacon top every hamlet and farm in all directions had its blaze. Gloucester cathedral was floodlit, and there appeared to be a firework display in progress in the park. Everywhere it seemed that everybody had chosen the same way to see off all the years of darkness by creating the biggest blaze they could build. It was an utterly unforgettable sight. Only in the few weeks previous to VE day had some street lighting been restored, otherwise on any other night since the summer of 1939 anybody standing on the beacon would not have seen a single light anywhere. Perfect weather bringing total clarity in the night air produced the most vivid memory I shall ever recall.

As we finally drifted away in small groups towards the village we could see the glow of all the fires in the villages and farms on the wolds to the east and south, the whole country as far as the eye could see in every direction was sharing the celebration. I had not been on the hill in the dark before, and I was fascinated to see for the first time the tiny lights of hundreds of glow-worms everywhere we walked.

Sadly there was another side to all the festivity. A number of people in the village, and boys at our school had been told of a dear relative killed in action. In addition some were prisoners of the Japanese, and from others nothing had been heard since their capture in the Far East. Moreover it was easy to think of the Pacific war as an American task, forgetting the British army still battling on through Burma.

With the long summer evenings now upon us the absence of black-out precautions was not very apparent, and in many respects life continued as before. There was no prospect of rationing ending for a long time to come, and apart from the need to defeat Japan everybody seemed very worried about how we were going to get on with Russia. I remained convinced that one day I would be called up.

Meanwhile it was hay making time. Down on the farm the tractor was taking the mower round and round each field until the last little island of standing grass in the middle lay with the rest. Rabbits running from the mower often headed for the middle of the field with the result that several had to make a dash for it on the final circuits. This was where Peter, the man we had first met ferreting, had a job to do. Armed with the old twelve bore that lodged on the cross-beam in the long shed he rode on the step of the tractor to shoot rabbits. I soon realised why nobody else wanted to use the farmer's old gun. The mechanism was so loose where it met the barrels that each time a shot was fired a burst of hot smoke flew from the junction of stock and barrel. Fortunately I never heard of anybody being injured using it.

A few days later the horses were brought out to pull spinners through the cut grass to toss it up for better drying. Then out came the wide horse drawn rake again which laid the hay in long rows from end to end of the field. We had watched carefully to learn how the horses were harnessed and backed into the shafts, soon we would be able to help the preparation and perhaps work that big rake.

Stacking involved everybody including ourselves, it was urgent work in case the weather failed. A pronged sledge mounted on the front of the tractor pushed quantities of hay across the field to the stack builders who forked it onto the rising pile. Behind came others with rakes and pitchforks gathering the grass that the tractor had missed. It was hot work, and the harvest mites were working at least as hard as the rest of us, biting anything they could get to. By lunch time the sun had come round onto the big stoneware cider jar that had been carefully placed in the shade of the hedge hours earlier, and the contents were well warmed. The adults passed the communal china mug round, and watched as we carefully tasted rough home-made cider for the first time.

It had a strangely complicated mixture of flavours, or so it seemed to me. Having never previously taken alcoholic drink I could not recognise what had happened to that rather tart apple juice.

Our neighbour had come home on leave again, and offered to take us both pike fishing. We boys did not possess pike tackle, but could fish for roach and perch while watching how to catch a pike. Turning off the main road up a muddy track beside a small stream we came to a group of red brick mill buildings stretching across the little valley. The far wall of these buildings was the dam beyond which spread the millpond. Like so many waters neglected during the war the banks were overgrown and in the upper reaches silt had left very little water. To our left there was a short stretch of clear bank beside an iron roofed open barn, and there we found the boat, flat bottomed with sloped ends rather like a small punt. Paddling out to a point midway across the lake and about fifteen yards from the dam we dropped our two anchor weights and set up float tackles for perch, casting close to the lily pads along the mill wall, while our neighbour threw a spinner towards the middle of the lake.

The water was beautifully clear, and in the bright sunshine one had to keep very still and quiet in order to avoid frightening the fish. We were told that anglers usually waited until autumn to fish for pike, after the summer weed growth had died back, but our friend had to take his opportunity. Around the far narrow end of the lake the tall overhanging willows and alders were full of small birds, while beneath moorhens walked carefully across the big floating leaves of the white water lilies. The summer air was full of insects and swallows constantly swooped across the water feeding.

Suddenly a pike struck, the stout rod bent, and a couple of minutes later, there was the biggest fish we had seen caught, a five pound pike. Carefully lifted out on the gaff it was quickly given a blow with the priest at the base of the skull which killed it. A spring gag in the great alligator like jaws enabled forceps to remove the treble hook and spinner. Just to keep it out of the way the pike was then dropped head first into a bucket, where it slipped down gradually into a U shape.

We had no great success with the perch that day, but the pike would be worth taking home. And now our education continued as our friend showed us how to prepare the fish. As in our home, his kitchen had its sink and draining area immediately against the long window looking out onto the yard. To prevent any unpleasant smells getting into the house the window was left wide open. Many hours after it was killed the pike was firmly set in its bucket shape, and now it was held on a board and its head cut off with a very sharp knife. Next it was slit up the underside from the vent and all its guts removed.

At this point it was necessary to wash out the interior under a running tap, scraping the last of the black blood out from beside the spine with a pointed knife. We were watching carefully, this was something we would be doing many times in the future, or so we hoped. The slippery carcase was held firmly by the shoulders in the bottom of the sink as this final act of the cleaning process was performed. Suddenly the body straightened, thrashed violently from side to side of the sink, and as we leapt back in alarm one flip of the tail took the fish through the open window and into the yard.

We had seen our first example of reflex action, something we have always remembered, caused in this case by accidentally turning the hot water tap on instead of cold.

# CHAPTER 8

Now at last, just a few weeks after VE day, father told us that we would be going for a summer holiday, the first since 1939. Our destination was a place called Dolgelley, near the west coast of Wales. Looking at my atlas I found it about half way up Wales, not far from the sea, with its own river. We were past sand castles now, fishing was what we wanted and this place ought to be ideal. The map showed a nearby lake and we could hope for some perch fishing even it the trout in the river proved difficult. Father had inherited some good trout rods from his late uncle, and he too would be wanting to try his hand at casting a fly.

Two firms in the village kept hire cars, though they were only given a limited petrol allowance. Father did not drive, nor did he own a car, and it was really quite remarkable that he was able to book Mr. Horne's big Austin to drive us all the way from Painswick to Dolgelley, and to call again to collect us a fortnight later. How he managed to arrange this I still do not know, but we had long since realised that where organisation was concerned father always knew what to do.

Sure enough, on the appointed morning there was the car at our door, Percy, the smartly uniformed chauffeur waiting to strap our cases on the rear carrier. Fishing rods were carefully tucked away and we set off on a wonderful drive towards and beyond the furthest westward mountains we could see from the beacon.

Through Gloucester and the lowland orchards we drove, gradually climbing after Hereford into more hilly country, and the journey seemed as if it would never end. Dear Percy never exceeded thirty miles per hour, whether to conserve fuel, or to avoid any recurrence of the car sickness that afflicted my brother long years earlier I do not know. Gradually the hills became steeper, the distant mountains higher until at last we could glimpse the sea far ahead. Eventually after running down through valleys set with tiny villages we saw to our right the little river where lower down we hoped to fish.

Dolgelley at last, only a little place, where the road went on to the seaside at Fairbourne, while another branched right over the arched river bridge to continue down the north bank to Barmouth. Just short of the bridge stood the square solid black and white mass of the Golden Lion Royal hotel, our home for the next two weeks, hardly a hundred yards from the river.

Cases were taken up to our rooms, Percy was thanked and lunched, and as he set off on his long run home we went down to the bridge to look at the river. Level sheep cropped grass banks topped a drop of four feet to a slope down to the river gravels, there was very little water, slightly more above the bridge where the flow was slower. We would never need to wade beyond the depth of our wellingtons. Back then to the tackle shop we had passed to buy our licences and a few assorted trout flies. Now at last we could fish, and the upstream stretch offered plenty of space where we could avoid getting in each other's way. Learning to cast a fly is a nasty tangly experience, oddly enough that extremely low summer level of water was ideal for our purpose, giving us wide open spaces to work in.

After a good deal of practice we occasionally caught a tiny trout, but there were plenty of other things to do and plenty of evidence that there were good fish to be had. Almost every evening fresh salmon was offered for dinner, the head waiter explaining that everybody was making the most of the situation before the keeper returned from the army next week. We admired some magnificent fish in that dining room, and soon afterwards we saw where most of them were taken.

We had all caught the bus to Barmouth, the little seaside

town at the mouth of the river, and soon after leaving Dolgelley had driven over another bridge, this spanning a different and bigger river than the Wnion we knew. Below that bridge was a great pool where the water circled slowly beneath the steep gravel banks, surely this must be the place where the big fish were caught.

At Barmouth newspaper placards proclaimed that an atomic bomb had been dropped on Japan. Father bought a paper, I was not really interested. The best it could mean would be some bigger and better bang that might end this horrible war sooner. I had no idea what atomic meant, and I was not inclined to spare it a thought.

After all, here we were on our first summer holiday away from home since the war began, and just as I did not expect to waste any of this precious time going to church, so I was certainly not going to spare time fretting about the war. That wonderful river pool just walking distance down the road from our hotel was now my only interest, that was where I would be to-morrow.

Barmouth had pleasant sand beaches sloping down in slices between heavy wooden barriers which gave a little shelter from the breeze. To our left a long railway viaduct spanned the mouth of the rivers, and beyond, on the far side, we could see more broad expanses of sand. I was no swimmer, and therefore unconcerned that bathing here was unsafe. The return bus journey gave another tantalising view of the bridge pool, we had to go fishing there the next day.

As soon as we could leave the breakfast table we gathered our small assortment of tackle and walked down the road to the bridge. At low summer level there was hardly any river flow coming through the arches, and we could stand on the bridge foundations from which the pool fell straight into deep water. We soon found the favourite local bait, somebody had left a box of very large striped worms on the bank and we tried our luck with some of them. We tried too with everything else we could think of, but no fish came near. The water was too clear and low, the sun too bright I suspect. This was an evening or night time pitch.

The tide flowed up river just as far as the bridge and it was easy to imagine how salmon would run up on the tide, and then have to wait in the pool until a storm brought sufficient river water to allow them to swim further up. This must be the place where the poachers were working their nets so successfully. Then at last we saw the ripple of a dorsal fin on the far side of the pool, some large fish was cruising just below the surface. We soon realised that there was something wrong with it as it turned and rolled in the water.

Back at the hotel we told the head waiter who confirmed that the poachers had dropped a fish off the gaff the previous night. The next day it was found bled to death and useless for eating, an eighteen pound sea trout.

With no prospect of rain that beautiful spot would yield no fish so we set about sampling some of the other new experiences the locality offered. Just up the road from Dolgelley was a mountain, Cader Idris, and having never climbed a mountain before this became our next objective. It was a fascinatingly varied walk. We followed a little lane up the hill from the town, distant views opening further and further as we went, until the roadway levelled out and there to our right we were looking down on a long, reed fringed lake, below the little hotel beside the road. Here our route turned leftward across open ground and up towards the mountain.

Quite unlike our familiar Cotswold hills, so hard and dry in summer, this walk found us all too often in well concealed patches of bog. The whole scale of things was vastly greater than anything we had met previously. Ahead a great vertical rock wall curved across our path, tumbling scree banked below it. As we approached that scree gradually changed from looking like the small stuff found in the old quarries around Painswick, and proved in fact to comprise sizeable boulders extending up the slope for hundreds of feet.

Finally we found our way up that route to the top, looking down into deep blue lakes, one on each side of the summit, many hundreds of feet below. Coming back down a different and easier track we were told on our return to the hotel that we had done the climb the wrong way round, and I had to admit that climbing down over the boulder bank would have been preferable to scaling it.

We had seen so many other mountains from the top of Cader Idris, and in the next few days went for bus trips towards some of those areas we had distantly glimpsed. The papers told of another atomic bomb being dropped on Japan, then of a probable Japanese surrender. At last came the news, to-morrow was to be VJ Day.

Now I really was going to enjoy my holiday. Had I been at home I would once again have been lugging timber up the beacon. Here in Dolgelley I could relax and enjoy whatever the local population arranged by way of celebration. The hotel dining room, with tall sash windows on three sides, looked out directly onto the public recreation ground beside the river. Here a huge bonfire was being built. The war with Germany having been finished a couple of months earlier a certain number of fireworks, mostly of military origin, had been acquired.

The very hot weather was obviously about to reach a spectacular climax. The air was still, great piles of black clouds were gathering, it was almost impossible to keep cool. Before going down to dinner my brother and I had opened the sash window of our room, the velvet curtains over the dining room windows were closed to keep out mosquitoes but the sashes behind them were wide open. We could hear a number of large fireworks exploding in the narrow streets. Then just as we were finishing our meal there was a loud bang beneath a nearby table, filling the room with smoke. A Thunderflash had been flung through the window and had rolled under the Bishop of Ely's table. Dashing upstairs to vent our laughter we found the bedroom curtains alight, another Thunderflash had been thrown through our open window. Obviously it was going to be a lively evening. Having put out the fire and closed the window we went out to join the crowds by the river.

The thunderstorm waited until the festivities were over before coming to tidy up the mess. It was nearing midnight when the rain started, and the thunder soon became deafening as each clap echoed back and forth between the surrounding mountain cliffs. The din was almost continuous for hours, I have never since heard a louder storm. This really was a memorable way to celebrate victory. The scene in the morning was incredible. The river, a trickle five feet below the field the previous evening, was running brown and bank high. In the night it had obviously risen much higher because every trace of the fire had been washed away. We heard of damage, bridges down further up river, but what a marvellous theatrical performance to mark the ending of the war.

Percy and the Austin duly returned, and long hours slowly driving home gave time for thoughts on the next school year.

Somewhere in the early dark years of the war a child had grown to boyhood, now suddenly another word was needed. In less than twelve months I must take the School Certificate examination, and unless I reached certain high standards the prospect of further advance to university would be blocked. It was a very worrying prospect indeed. School breaks in future would not be occupied by throwing and catching balls or joking in groups; now we would all join those we had seen each earlier year, who with bowed shoulders strolled around, open book in hand, honing their learning for the struggle ahead. One war might now be over, for the fifth form it was just beginning. So sobering was the prospect that it was as if by adding responsibility to boyhood our condition had irreversibly altered. Another definition was needed which I could not find. Youth is probably the only suitable word.

This year we would be taught by the senior staff, great men of whom we had lived in dread while in the lower forms, now to be found human, expert and amazingly capable of pushing into us quantities of knowledge we would never have thought ourselves able to absorb. Homework requirements increased enormously, and the need for space and peace in which to complete it underlined most forcibly the fact that our home was far too small.

The black-out shutters had gone at last, but nobody seemed very sure when the next war would break out. We all kept up our work with the army cadets, certain that sooner or later we would be called up. Here too there were qualifications to be earned, the two parts of War Certificate A might well be worth having later. Wooden rifles had been replaced by the long Ross, and now the armoury beside the woodwork shop received a supply of the .303 short Lee-Enfield. At last we had the same gun that serving soldiers were using. Beautifully balanced, it made arms drill much easier.

Where shooting was concerned we were still restricted to the .22 ranges, and again I took every opportunity to practice in the village skittle alley. From this contact a useful source of pocket money arose. Painswick Institute started to play skittles matches, and a couple of lads were needed to replace the fallen pins during home matches. My brother and I made sure we were given a chance, and by showing speed and accuracy we kept the job.

At Christmas time age at last qualified me for another chance to earn a little pocket money, helping to deliver the post. It was a wonderful new experience, though very hard work. Walking into the Post Office before dawn, well wrapped in mackintosh, scarf and gloves, I found the postmaster and three regular postmen sorting cards, letters and packets. The stove made the small room very hot, and I wondered how uncomfortable the postmen must be in their heavy serge uniforms, though they seemed contented enough. I did not know whether their ruddy complexions were due to the stove, or to the harsh weather they so frequently had to contend with.

Over the years I had become fairly familiar with the layout of the village and surrounding area, now I was given a number of bundles, each tied with string, which had been sorted into the correct order for the route I was to take. With the big canvas bag over my shoulder I walked out into the cold street. Gloves proved useless and soon went into the bag, I had noticed that the regular postmen used fingerless mittens, and leafing through a bundle of letters they were really the only sensible protection from the cold. Having delivered my little load, nearly all of it to the right places, it was time to go back to the Post Office for the packets and registered post. The first batch had all been small enough to pass through the letter box, now I must ring the door bell.

Many parcels were bulky, wrapped in thick brown paper and tied with string, red sealing wax on the knots, others a small hessian sack tied with a label at the neck might contain a brace of pheasants. To deliver all these around and beyond the village required more than a canvas bag, now it was time to take out the Post Office bicycle with its big carrier frame on the front. That machine was terribly heavy, and could really only be ridden downhill, but it would carry a lot of parcels which could then be pushed rather than carried by the pusher.

This was much harder work than the first round, often taking me far up the Cheltenham road or across the valley to Edge or Bulls Cross. Either of the last two meant a very steep climb back up the hill to the Post Office.

Then in the gathering dusk I would find that a couple of telegrams needed to be delivered to outlying houses, another bicycle job, but first check that the battery lights are working. It was strange to pull the bell at some great remote house and be asked by the maid to wait in case there was a reply to send. It was not the reply that concerned me, rather it was the tip. An extra sixpence, or perhaps with luck a shilling would make a long day more profitable. Of course the job ended on Christmas Eve, but it was an experience I would not have wanted to miss.

There was more than enough homework to fill the winter evenings, and now, at the start of 1946, the pressure increased and study spilled over into the week-ends. There was still firewood gathering to be done, and not much time left for leisure. I had been fortunate in being allowed to occasionally borrow a .177 BSA target air rifle, and sitting in the stack yard at the farm for just an hour or so gave excellent sport with the rats.

Then too there was the forge where we made grappling hooks to clear summer pond weed. We had met a boy who we had not known earlier because he went to school in Cheltenham. Behind his home was a disused blacksmith's forge, where we were surprised to find stocks of fuel and iron rod, anvil, tongs and hammers, even the bellows to blow the fire. We had no need to make horseshoes, but the thought of clearing fishing channels in the local lakes in summer soon had us hammering a point on a length of iron rod, bending it round like a giant fish-hook, then bending a ring by which we would be able to fix a rope to the hook. Since the end of the war new experiences were crowding in, many depending on the expanded horizons provided by my bicycle.

I had heard years before of the daffodil fields at Newent, though few would have had time to visit then during the war. This spring it seemed everybody was going to go there. One sunny Saturday I cycled over to Gloucester and joined by far the largest crowd I had ever seen. Thousands of bicycles were being ridden along the Newent road, three or four abreast as far as the eye could see. This was no race, the pace was leisurely, family groups rode together without children trying to beat their elders. The whole procession must have continued for hours, fortunately on Saturday there was hardly any motor traffic in either direction.

Soon we found the flowers. The bright green spring pastures, often bounded by hazel spinneys were thickly dotted with the little yellow blooms, and everywhere people were leaning their cycles against the hedge, climbing over gates and picking as many daffodils as they could carry. There seemed to be miles of these fields, there was no need to stop at the first, there might be better flowers a little further on. I suppose I picked about as many as the rest of us, I came home with four bunches hanging from my handlebars, six in my saddle bag, and four more tied to my rear carrier. If anything the return procession, slightly slower, was an even more extraordinary sight than the outward ride.

The lack of space at home had long been a problem, now it was becoming a serious nuisance. Father worked late at his little office in Stroud, I stayed on after school to do homework and revision. So far as my brother and I were concerned we had been looking for a house in the village for years, at different times we had seen every possible home in the area, but only one appealed to us. We would stand in the sunken lane looking through the bottom of the big privet hedge hiding it from the road. It was a modern double fronted house facing south towards Stroud, with large gardens, and two garages. Obviously it offered much more room than our little terrace house so crushed between its neighbours that its window bays squeezed out onto the pavement.

The exams were fast approaching, and thoughts of houses had to be set aside, the only relaxation now was the occasional fishing trip. A friend from Stroud introduced me to a long narrow lake off the Chalford valley, reed banked along one side, the other overhung with beech trees. The water was very shallow and there were few positions from which to cast except a little narrow jetty. It was a wonderful place on a sunny Saturday afternoon after a short cycle ride approach. The reeds were full of small birds, dragonflies dashed urgently around, and the perch were happy to accept the little red worms my hook presented. The sport was good, but very small floats were needed because of the shallow water. Apart from the usual moorhens, coots and mallard, a number of snakes could be seen swimming out from the woodland side in the heat of the afternoon, hunting frogs and toads presumably, but ready to bag chicks from the nests in the reed bed opposite as well I supposed. It was a warm peaceful place where we could try to forget the threat of examinations for a couple of hours.

Our neighbour, now home from the war, was very helpful in introducing me to the owners of other lakes. One in particular I remember well. Deep in the woods at Cranham, it had not been fished or maintained through the long course of the war. Previously it had held trout. I went to have a look at it. The little bungalow seemed unoccupied, reeds lined two sides, thick bushes blocked a third, a small boat landing stage left the last side fishable. A number of domestic ducks had the run of the place, with the result that the water was muddy. I saw no trout rise, and assumed that the best bait would be a small red worm.

Now the examinations were upon us. If we were to progress further it was not a question of gaining passes in our subjects, we must obtain at least five credit grades, two of which had to be in English language and Mathematics. The English language paper was the really critical one because here we would be presented with a list of titles from which we must choose one on which to write our essay. We lived in hope that a title would appear about which we could write something.

The examination timetable showed the English literature paper in the morning of the first day, the afternoon free, then the vital English language paper the following morning. We would all be cramming the English literature books furiously before the paper, then ready to relax completely in the afternoon as there was nothing one could prepare for the essay paper the next day.

For the exams the gymnasium was filled with widely spaced desks and in the very hot summer weather we all perspired under its iron roof. After the first paper had been handed in I had planned to cycle with my angling friend, Alan, to that pond in Cranham woods. The sun was very hot, but once off our bicycles we could feel a little breeze ruffling the beech leaves, though the pond with its shielding reeds was flat calm. The only movement came from the ducks, which left when we offered them no food.

No fish were rising, in the hot high sunshine they were probably lazing in the deeper water. Float tackle and a small worm did not seem to excite much interest, but we could relax in the deep silence of the wood, watching finches, tits and warblers around the pond. At last a float dipped and a half-pound trout was caught, followed by another couple.

We must not stay late, bearing in mind the need to be fresh for that next exam, and that Alan had four miles further to ride before he reached home than I would travel. I had caught my first sizeable trout, making it a very memorable day.

Next morning we took our places for the English language paper, my desk to the far right of the gym, Alan's toward the left. Of course none of us was allowed to speak. The invigilator distributed the question papers, face down, one to each desk, returned to his place at the front and, checking the time, told us to begin. A quick glance at the essay subjects had Alan and I exchanging joyful grins, there in the middle of the title options was 'A Saturday Afternoon in the Country'.

That ride up the lush tree-lined valley to Painswick, the pretty Cotswold village, the views from the high route further on, cycling through the great beechwoods at the valley end, the old stone track to the silent bungalow with its cottage garden flowers, the birds, and then the trout, had given us sufficient material to write half a dozen essays under that title. Later we felt we had really done justice to that great bogy paper.

Over the next ten days many more tests had be tackled, but before that came great excitement at home. Father had bought a house, the very one which my brother and I had so admired, and we would move in on the last day of term. Now at last we could look at it properly, noticing that though double fronted, it was in fact L shaped. A wing containing the kitchen and pantries, with a double bedroom and second bathroom above, served by a back staircase was designed to accommodate the resident maid. The view we had seen from the road was of the through drawing room to the right, dining room to the left, with two double bedrooms and bathroom above, one single room over the front door and another over the side entrance.

Parking removal vans presented no difficulty, the five barred gate to the left opened onto a wide gravelled parking area, the drive extending to the big timber garage, and continuing to a smaller one at the top of the garden. Between these stood a tool shed and a fruit storage shed. Furniture and possessions I had long since forgotten, contents of our old London home, were brought from storage. Uncle David's lovely Bluthner grand piano found a decent home at last in the drawing room, with father's enormous armchair. The heavy oak extending table fitted nicely into the dining room with the big black sideboard, while oil portraits of various ancestors looked down as I had last seen them when I was only eight years old. Even the monochrome Landseer print of a stable scene which had hung in our kitchen play area in London returned to a place in the hall.

The transfer did not pass entirely smoothly. Chips the cat disappeared a couple of days after we moved in. Mother thought she had probably returned to her old home. Lately the cat had once again become fat and ugly, a condition usually followed by yet another litter of kittens. She was found under the rain water butt at the old address, and brought back with her newly arrived brood to learn to accept her new surroundings.

Our new home was completely different from the house in New Street. Now we had all the space we could ever need, no traffic passing just outside the windows, views now to the south and west rather than the eastward aspect, dominated by the parish church, which had been our limit for the past six years.

Since father did not drive, the big garage became our workshop, here at last we could repair bicycles and use grandfather's old bench and carpentry tools to try our hand at skills, where previously we had been restricted to working a bit of wood held in the hand with a clasp knife. There was of course another side to living in such spacious surroundings. It took a couple of hours each week in the summer to cut the three lawns, and father was not expecting to have to do that with two strapping lads in the family. Hedge cutting was a hard day's work twice a year, another job for my brother and I. We never came near to mastering the ground elder in the herbaceous borders, but the big beds of the vegetable garden had to be dug and regularly weeded. It was almost as if leisure time was now available only on wet or winter week-ends.

There were some exceptions however. A number of events, suspended during the war, were now returning. All of course were new experiences to me, as when I accompanied father to a county cricket match at Gloucester. Now at last allowed to play myself, I had enjoyed games at school the previous term, though I would never be a first eleven performer. Sitting quietly in my deck chair just behind the front row of famous names of earlier years in their blazers and Panama hats, I soon realised how boring cricket could be unless you really studied the subtleties of the play. Yet out there were men who had played for England, and some who still did. I watched in the hope of learning, but the hard seats and the sun in my eyes were discouraging. At the close of a long day's play I had found little excitement, and as the bus took us home I thought of what else I could have done with my precious Saturday.

A more compelling attraction was the return of the Cheltenham cricket festival, including a match between Gloucestershire and the first visiting touring side since the war, the Indians. Played on the beautiful Cheltenham College ground, this was certainly worth my Saturday to watch the opening day. The bus would reach the College long before the start of play, and we planned to stay on board to the terminus just behind the Promenade, look at the shops, and then stroll along to the ground.

The weather was looking very threatening, and as the bus approached Cheltenham black clouds were piling up all around us. We had walked as far as the Promenade when a great thunderstorm cleared the streets. Standing in the entrance of Austin Reed's shop we watched as everybody dashed for cover in doorways and shops. In a minute or so the raindrops were splashing up feet above the ground, the torrent roaring just less loudly than the thunder. Soon the whole width of the Promenade was a single river, flowing fast from above the Queen's hotel, down the length of the road and into the front door of Boots. We wondered what the Indians would think of Cheltenham. There could be no cricket, and when at last the downpour eased we walked back to the bus station and returned home.

The move to our new home prevented any summer holiday travel that year, but all the novelty of settling in helped to take my mind off the awful question of exam results. Striding round behind the new Atco motor mower kept me occupied for hours. Somehow father never mastered the knack of starting the thing, and of course, once I had managed to get it going it was I who had to hang on to the throttle and follow the machine in case it stopped.

# CHAPTER 9

At last the examination results became known, I had obtained the necessary grades to move on to studies for Higher Certificate, a two year sixth form course, and my friends had been similarly successful. Those Higher Certificate grades would determine whether or not we might be offered university places.

Meanwhile we had reached a parting of ways. Sixth form study followed one of two routes, known as Arts or Science. We had all studied the same subjects to School Certificate level, now we must choose between a course extending our range in languages, or one devoted to science subjects, Physics, Chemistry and Mathematics. My results had shown the same level in all subjects, but I was certainly not inclined to pursue a science course. Arts had to be my choice, and having studied English, French and Latin I would now have to attempt to master German also, in just two years.

For a short time before the start of the new school year the tension was relieved and I could start to appreciate the new home and enjoy a few cycle trips and fishing expeditions. To sit by some quiet lake watching a little float, and the ripples on the water, the birds, animals and insects, without regard for the passage of time was a wonderful relaxation. I no longer had to keep looking at a watch to ensure that I did not miss my bus home, there beside me lay my bicycle.

Remembering the cycle trip to Newent I realised that other interesting places were now within range, and one fine day a group of us went to Ross on Wye. It was a memorable ride, fairly level at first beyond Gloucester, then climbing up through the woods above Huntley before reaching the long run down to Ross and its beautiful stretch of the Wye. The afternoon journey home was very hot, and we were glad to stop in the hills before Huntley to enjoy ginger beer out of stone bottles at the little Farmer's Boy inn.

At home we were settling into our new surroundings, remembering that there would no longer be a resident maid, nor the full-time gardener who had been employed by the previous owner. My room looked out to westward past the bungalow next door with its walnut tree and chicken run, over the valley to the huts of Paul Camp and the brown scarred flank of Scottsquarry hill, showing bare tracks where the Churchill tanks had been tested during the war.

The quiet was wonderful so far from the main street, and only a few yards from the open farmland in the valley below. Study would be far less liable to distraction now in the next critical couple of years. Not that I expected to be working too intensely at first, after one examination year it would be only natural to relax the pressure a little for a few months at least.

I had long been aware of the strange fact that at school one knew the names of the senior boys, but that as you graduated to the upper forms you could not name those in more junior classes. This was not just a case of looking up to people, rather it reflected the fact that these seniors performed various duties as prefects or as heads of house or team captains whereby they became more widely known. I had to face the fact that I would not be able to work quietly through my lower six form year, but might well be called upon to take on duties of various sorts, particularly since those in their final year were usually excused from distractions from study. I hoped that I could continue my still rather shy existence without having to sacrifice too much of my precious leisure time, nor have to devote my lunch breaks to patrolling the school grounds on the look-out for miscreants.

My hopes were most rudely dashed, I was singled out

for terrible exposure. The new headmaster had decided to revive a pre-war school custom of producing a play. His choice was *Charles the King*, a chronicle on the life of Charles 1. It involved nearly fifty acting parts with many others employed as stagehands. To my absolute horror I was cast as the king.

How I came to be chosen for this remains a mystery, though it was suggested that the headmaster's wife, as make-up supervisor, had decided that she could make me look like the well known Van Dyck portrait of the king. I had never acted before, the nearest I had come to opening my mouth in public was an occasional contribution to a discussion in the school debating society. Now here was a play of thirteen scenes in many of which I had a major role. Not only were there an enormous number of lines to be memorised, but in addition I would then have to deliver them on stage, and to several audiences. Worst of all was a scene where standing alone I would deliver a long speech to the audience.

Swept along by an interminable succession of rehearsals, concentration on memorising lines left little room for my fears. Then at last the whole business took a big messy step nearer reality when the costumes from the original London production arrived in great hampers, and the time had come for dress rehearsals. What extraordinary clothes people used to wear. I was expected to perform in tights and frilly bottomed breeches with tin buckles concealing the laces of my school shoes. They stuck false hair on my chin, rubbed nasty grease over my face and neck, then adding colour with thick oily make-up pencils, before topping out their handiwork with a great wig.

The wig was horribly hot, but there was no time to hate the whole wretched business, right up to the start I had to concentrate continually on polishing my lines. Then too there were several rapid dress changes to be made between scenes, until at last I tottered alone onto the stage under an enormous cloak which had required the combined strength of two dressers to hoist it onto my shoulders, to deliver my speech to the audience. Even after my execution I could not clean up, because I had to resurrect and take my place in line for the curtain calls.

What relief I felt as I ripped that beard hair off my chin for the last time and rubbed yet more oily cream into my skin to get rid of all the make-up. I still felt disgusting until I had managed to have several good washes with hot water and soap. Compensations began to appear. No longer having to remember lines I was able to feel pleased by the local newspaper reports of the play, where I found complimentary mentions of my performance. If ever I had to act again I would be less aghast at the prospect after that initial experience, nor could I possibly be given such a long and demanding role.

More than half way to Christmas I had hardly touched my study books that autumn term, though I felt it should be possible to catch up on work over the next five terms. I still had no idea how I would eventually earn my living, and the thought certainly crossed my mind that acting was an option if I had really performed as well as the kind newspaper reports suggested. In the dark evenings I started on a spell of concentrated reading, in the congenial conditions of my own quiet room at home. The literature element of Higher Certificate English and French comprised a large number of books, but by the time Christmas approached I felt I was making useful progress.

Then late one evening I heard the click of the drive gate, and wondering who was there went downstairs to the kitchen.

No visitor was expected, and the street light further down the lane left our drive in darkness, but somebody had come in, and hearing the gate click again as I reached the back door I knew that they had quickly gone again. Switching on the outside light I opened the door to look down the drive, not noticing at first the package that had been left on the doorstep. Wrapped neatly in fresh greaseproof paper was a very big table-dressed chicken.

Mother and father, listening to the wireless on the other side of the house had heard nothing, but did not take long to guess what was happening. Rationing was still very much a part of our lives but the arrival of this chicken was not so much the work of Father Christmas as that of the Inspector of Taxes.

I came to realise that after the war many small farmers who had never kept proper accounts found themselves suddenly faced with years of back assessments. As an accountant father had taken on a number of such farmers as clients, and had succeeded in negotiating with the Inspector on their behalf. He also introduced them to a simple and acceptable accounting procedure for the future. Several later told me that they literally saw father as saving their businesses. That magnificent bird, now sitting on the great cold stone slabs of the larder, was a thank offering. We quickly realised that others might attempt that dark approach, or the narrow path to the front door, and made sure that the next night, Christmas Eve, the outside lights were left on at the front and side doors.

One or two brought gifts to father's office, but the rest all left theirs without even ringing the bell, not for them to call uninvited on their professional adviser. There came a sack of apples, a tray of eggs, another chicken, and a big piece of home cured bacon that Christmas, and fortunately the custom continued for several years. Most of the givers were eventually identified, some never owned up. Our home had not seen a turkey on the table since before the war, but those chickens were delicious.

Again I had supplemented my pocket money delivering the Christmas post, the weather now far worse than the previous year, but my earnings bought a pike rod and reel, extending my scope in fishing terms to the really big fighters. Snow brought out the big elm sledge again, we were now quite capable of hauling it up the hill, and made good use of it that holiday hurtling down the well packed surface of the cemetery run, leaping over the dips that crossed it. Our sledge was now one of the fastest in the village, its steel shod runners well polished by use.

Unfortunately snow did not just mean fun. An unusually cold 1947 winter combined with a fuel shortage and power cuts must have left mother wondering whether it would not have been easier to keep a smaller house from freezing up. Certainly my new pike fishing outfit would have to wait for easier conditions. Winter was indeed the time for pike fishing, but not in weather as severe as this. Snowfalls followed in quick succession until finally in the last week of March a general thaw brought great floods to the Severn valley. In Gloucester I remember standing in Westgate Street beside the cathedral approach with floodwater almost to the steps of the Shire Hall and the west door of the cathedral.

Somehow we still managed to get to school and back through all this, and although inter-house music and dramatic competitions had now been introduced I successfully pleaded that having lost so much ground the previous term I should be excused from involvement. Nevertheless I was persuaded to take a big part in a Painswick production of Sheridan's The Critic during the Easter holiday. This acting business was beginning to come rather more easily, though I never really felt comfortable in costume.

We helped with the haymaking that summer, earning a swig from the big cider jar at lunch time, and a shandy at the Cross Hands at the end of the day. Mrs. Garraway did not notice our age, and we were able to learn how shove ha'penny and table skittles were played in that little pub she kept.

Father had arranged a family summer holiday at Cardigan. Farther south than Dolgelley on the same west Wales coast, Cardigan too had its river, the Teifi famed for sea trout. Once again Mr. Horne's Austin was booked, and the smartly liveried Percy drove us sedately across Wales to the Black Lion hotel. The scenery was beautiful, and long before we reached our destination the road had entered the Teifi valley, following that very inviting river all the way to Cardigan.

Our hotel was a typical old coaching inn standing right beside the town bridge over the river, its entrance arch giving onto an inner courtyard. I remember that courtyard well as home to a large number of assorted cats. The dangers of interbreeding were all too evident, several of these animals showed congenital defects.

Trout fishing opportunities were rather limited. The river was tidal at Cardigan, and for a couple of miles upstream, but beyond were places where we could cast a fly after a short bus journey. The river was low, this was high summer, and we caught no trout. There were other attractions a bus ride away, beaches and little seaside villages along the coast. There were also a number of boatmen taking small parties down river from Cardigan bridge to the sea to look at the wild sheep on Cardigan Island, just offshore, and the great fold cliffs with their sea caves to the southward. They had one difficulty to overcome, where river met sea there lay a sand bar impassable at low tide.

One afternoon Mr. Bowen took us out in his boat Dancer. A long slim skiff like craft, she had a small inboard engine amidships, and was otherwise simply an open boat. As we neared the bar our skipper turned Dancer about, moved all of us into the front end to raise his stern, then putting the engine into reverse let his propeller slowly cut a channel through the shallows until we reached deeper water.

The tide being low, the vertical cliffs of Cardigan Island presented a wet black rock wall hung with seaweed concealing many crab holes. We were shown how crabs could be taken by hand provided the arm was kept well up to the top of the hole out of claw reach until the creature could be seized from behind, since crabs always face the entrance to their hole. The technique was demonstrated and one large crab joined us to sit sulking in a wooden box as we turned southward. A couple of mackerel spinners were trailed, and we each caught several. There was a separate box for mackerel, but one was dropped beside the crab which promptly caught hold of the fish and in one claw movement chopped it in half. I decided that the skipper's method of catching crabs was far too chancy for my liking, though in fact he still had ten fingers despite having used that system for many years.

We began to run down past the fold cliffs and sea caves, with deep water right up to the rocks at this point. Close in under the cliffs a fisherman in another open boat was clearing his lobster pots. We lay off a little and stopped to see whether he had caught anything. He had cut out his engine and was keeping position by holding the float on the pot. At length he let go and went to start the engine. There was a little difficulty, he had to raise the engine cover and fumble inside, meanwhile the boat slowly revolved, drifting nearer to the boulders at the cliff bottom

Suddenly the engine started and the boat shot forward towards the cliffs, running up half way out of the water between two large boulders. That unfortunate fisherman, head down under the engine cover, had not noticed that his boat had turned, and now he had to leap out over the bow, give a mighty shove, and then take a yet more urgent leap to get back on board before finally bringing the situation under control. Those great fold cliffs give a marvellous echo, and though I could not understand a word he said it was obvious that he was swearing in Welsh with a fine fluency and truly operatic volume.

The poor chap had made our day, we laughed all the way back to Cardigan. Once again we had enjoyed a new experience, catching our first mackerel on spinners, now another novel episode quickly followed. The husbands of three other couples staying at the hotel were planning an evening duck shooting. My brother and I were asked if we would beat for them. Assuming that this meant an early evening wander through the reed beds above Cardigan bridge we agreed, but in fact this was to be an after dinner expedition, going by car some miles inland to a little heather covered hill, on top of which, we were told, we would find a dew pond.

One of the men knew this place, also that when we approached the pond the ducks roosting there would fly down to the river, over the three guns. It was a hot evening, and as my brother and I toiled up the hill I was glad to be wearing cool shorts. The result was rather disappointing, there were not many ducks, and after hearing a few distant bangs we started back down the hill. A few minutes later we saw the flash of a gun far below and spun round just in time to hear the spent shot whistling through the heather before it stung us behind our bare knees. We were later told very apologetically that one of the guns had fired at a curlew, forgetting that it was over our return path.

The leader now said that he would demonstrate how to kill a winged duck. One of us was to hold out the butt of an unloaded gun so that it presented a horizontal surface. The duck would be grasped around the body and brought sharply down in such a way that its neck struck across the gun butt, the neck being broken as the head came down beyond the butt. The demonstration went horribly wrong, the head struck full against the butt and the three of us were splattered with blood, brains and bits of bone. The gun butt was wiped and we returned to the hotel, avoiding that group for the rest of our stay. We had learned what spent shot felt like, and how not to kill a duck.

It had been an interesting holiday visiting so many new places, and following another slow scenic drive home we were in time to help with the harvest. The big paddle blades of the binder pushed the standing corn into the knives, a belt carrying the cut corn to a device that tied it in sheaves before dumping them behind the binder with its towing tractor. Then came the manual work, five sheaves at a time had to be set up in stooks like the ridge of a roof, three sheaves one side and two on the other, so arranged that the prevailing wind would blow between them, drying the straw. Remember not to get too close to Peter with that dreadful old twelve bore in case a rabbit comes out of the steadily shrinking corn cover.

After a few dry days came the pitchfork work, piling all those stooks onto carts and taking them to the farm, to be stacked in the Dutch barn until the threshing contractor's machine arrived to separate the grain from the straw. Several weeks waiting was involved as there were far more farmers with grain to thresh than there were contract machines. Then at last the great steam traction engine arrived towing the big red thresher.

The new school year had begun, and once again I found myself chosen to act a leading part in a play later that term. *The Importance of Being Earnest*, by Oscar Wilde was very different from the previous production. The cast was small, the lines magnificent, the costume no more outlandish than morning dress tails. I was now more at ease on stage, the last vestiges of my shyness almost erased, acting could well become my chosen career. The village had acquired its own international celebrity, the film star Phyllis Calvert had bought a house there, only a hundred yards up the lane from ours. Having one's own real live film star for a neighbour somehow tended to persuade me that anything was possible, if I eventually did attempt a stage career. Suddenly we had a great new game, people spotting, as Phyllis Calvert often had week-end visitors some of whom were starlets and some producers.

Meanwhile the final rehearsals were approaching, and all the cast were greatly looking forward to the performances, delivering Wilde's delicious lines and munching genteel little cucumber sandwiches. Unfortunately the outcome was less relaxed than I had hoped due to an incident at the final dress rehearsal. The climax of the play, in the third act, has a performer entering, carrying a rather shabby old holdall with the line "is this the handbag, Miss Prism?". At the dress rehearsal he said "is this the prism, Miss Handbag?". Through each performance we all sweated blood lest he make the same mistake again. Fortunately he was word perfect throughout.

Studies and other interests were reducing the time I could spend with the cadets, but I had passed War Certificate A parts 1 and 2. National Service was waiting for school-leavers, eighteen months in uniform, though this could be deferred for those in higher education. Having no idea of what future career to follow I had decided to do my conscripted time as soon as I had gained Higher Certificate unless a university place offered. I intended to work hard at National Service, a good record could be useful when returning to civilian life, In particular I wanted to learn to drive. Possession of the two parts of War Certificate A would be a useful start when official selection procedures began to sort out a new group of recruits. I could score one more small point by successfully completing what was called an initiative and endurance test. This involved two cadets being given a fairly distant destination to reach and return in forty eight hours without spending more than two shillings.

In late October two of us went to Stroud police station at six o'clock one Friday evening, had our cards signed and set out to travel to Dover and return by Sunday evening. We wore battledress with anklets and boots, greatcoats and berets, and we still felt the cold an hour or so later. We reasoned that our best chance of getting some really long lifts would be to make first for Cheltenham and the A40 traffic from South Wales. We were right, and after two lifts we were picked up at Andoversford by a flatbed lorry which took us all the way to Waterloo station on our route out of London. It was a very cold and uncomfortable ride, sitting with our backs to the cab, bouncing painfully up and down at each irregularity in the road.

The only free overnight accommodation was on the benches in the station concourse, most had already been taken by real servicemen. We bought coffee at the stall at the entrance and curled up for the night. Sleep was almost impossible due to the continual rattle of long lines of baggage trucks towed along by little tractors, and before daylight we set off down the Dover road. We were very fortunate and our cards were timed in at Dover police station at ten past ten in the morning. At that rate we could have completed the test in less than twenty four hours.

Having reached our objective so quickly we decided that since the weather looked fine we would follow a route along the south coast towards Southampton. A difficult day with a number of short lifts found us running out of daylight between Portsmouth and Fareham. The only cover we could find was a concrete pill-box from the war years. It was damp and dirty, and very cold. Once again we had little sleep. On Sunday morning there was hardly any traffic, but eventually we reached Salisbury, then Bath, and finally Stroud police station just before half past two in the afternoon. A uniformed figure at the roadside thumbing a lift was hardly ever refused, and in spite of the very scant traffic we achieved our objective. We also managed to keep within our cash limit because on more than one occasion a driver gave us money for food, and on Sunday morning a retired officer who picked us up took us to his home for breakfast.

The pike fishing season had now arrived. Already in the summer we had tried live baiting at Woodchester park, but the little roach attached to the two treble hooks of its Jardine snap tackle had pulled the big float along until it reached a convenient water lily, where it had swum round the stem. We had caught a lot of lily stems and lost a lot of small roach that day. At least we had learned why pike fishing is a winter sport, and now that the water weeds had all died down we could try some proper fishing.

Harry Grist's millpond at Woodchester was quite small, but reputed to contain good fish, and for the next few years it was our favourite lake. It was always fascinating to watch the big red float bobbing along, the waxed flax line floating behind over the dark mirror of the now weedless surface. Few singing birds remained now, moorhens only foraged along the margins, it was time of deep quiet.

The float had gone, the line was running out fast, time to grab the rod, set the ratchet and strike. The silence was broken by the chatter of the check, the smooth surface churning with the struggles of the fish until eventually it was sufficiently exhausted to be brought to the gaff. Unlike anything we had caught before this was a fish that could do one serious injury. Granted that the dorsal fin of a perch, and the spine on its gill cover were a nasty hazard, but it could be held in a cloth and kept under control. The pike on the other hand had a huge mouth with very nasty teeth capable of grabbing and swallowing fish and moorhens, we had even heard of a man who lost a hand after getting too close to a pike.

It was a job for gag and priest. First the priest to deliver a hefty blow to the base of the skull, then the spring gag to open the mouth and reveal the position of the hooks. A long metal rod with a notch in the end could push the hooks free, then the catch had to be put in a place where it could do no harm if it suddenly decided it was only stunned rather than dead. Pike fishing, we realised could involve a lot of waiting in cold conditions, but provided ample compensation in the thrill of catching one of these great predators.

I was now the proud possessor a Webley Mark 1 air pistol, a wonderful tool for killing rats. The day they threshed the corn provided excellent sport as the stack gradually reduced. Three men on the high platform at the back of the machine cut the twine binding the sheaves, dropping the corn into the great revolving drum which would separate the grain from the straw and chaff. I had to keep well away from the long drive belt hanging from the thresher to the steam traction engine which provided power for its operation. I killed plenty of rats but probably made little impression on the total rat population of those farm buildings.

# CHAPTER 10

This had been the year for my brother to take his School Certificate examinations, and despite gloomy predictions from a few of his masters he confounded the sceptics and obtained the necessary grades to enable him to join the Conway training ship after Christmas to study for a career in the Merchant Navy. He had been enchanted by the writings of John Masefield, not least his book on the Conway. Moreover his contact with the stresses of family life and father's unpredictable moods would now be limited to school holidays.

For me the change brought a considerable increase in gardening duties since chores could no longer be shared, and as younger brother spread his wings it became more urgent for me to seriously consider my future career. Though now past my seventeenth birthday I still had no idea how most people earned a living, nor what professional work entailed. I was certain on one point only, that I would not become a Chartered Accountant. To start my young adult life clerking in father's office was not an acceptable proposition.

Before my brother's departure in January 1948 we made one more pike fishing visit to Grists millpond. The weather was very cold and we were anxious not to waste precious time and daylight catching bait. The trout fishery off the Horsley road sold small deformed specimens for use as pike bait, and we therefore took the bus to Nailsworth and carried our tackle and bait can up to the fishery to buy half a dozen small trout. Then we dashed back to the bus station refreshing the water in the can before boarding for the journey back to the mill approach. Running up the track we found the lake frozen over, the little pike boat sunk at its moorings, and we smashed a hole in the ice to put our trout, now in a keep-net, where they could recover from the journey.

We baled out the boat and checked that it would float properly, then paddled it across the pond breaking the ice cover in two halves. Gradually over the next half hour the strong west wind blew the ice from the top of the lake under the sheet at the mill end, and we now had half a lake to fish in. We paddled out beside the ice fringe and cast our live-bait tackles. Despite the wintry conditions we had a good day and caught the bus home with four fish in a hessian sack which we left in the luggage compartment under the stair of the double decker. Watching floats had soon become too cold a pastime and for the last couple of hours we had been keeping warm by casting spinners.

Our catch presented a little problem, we had no inclination to eat pike, and the cat would never consume all that we had caught. I knew that the French ate pike, and perhaps some of the villagers would appreciate some. There came a cutting-up ceremony. Father had telephoned some of the friends he met at the village club, Bert Strange the postmaster, Horace Hollister the schoolmaster, Eddie Tidmarsh the butcher and George Fryer the grocer. All these expressed an interest and so it was on George Fryer's counter that those fish were cut up in suitable lengths for each family, or their cats as the case may have been.

My brother having now left, my pastimes turned more to guns. In the country it is inevitable that two people, however careful, make more noise than one. Now I could stalk as I wished without wondering whether it was he or I that the quarry had seen or heard before bolting. There was one place where this was especially important. At the side of the farm was a little feed mill, the upper floor with its hopper linked to the ground floor, where stood the milling machine, by a ladder fixed vertically in a corner of the wall. At the top of the ladder a trap door hinged up against the wall, in the space behind that door was a rat hole.

Entering the door of the mill very quietly, rats could be

heard moving around on the floor above. Holding the cocked pistol at eye level, and the ladder rungs in my left hand I climbed slowly up until I could see across the upper floor. At once they spotted me and I had the frightening experience of seeing a big rat running straight at my face until it swerved behind the trap door cover. Pistol held at eye level gave me one chance of a shot, but the action was too rapid for real accuracy.

I had become so accustomed to stalking prey to short range using a catapult that I found the pistol quite sufficient for ratting and rabbiting. Nevertheless I was keeping up my rifle skills at the .22 ranges, and was now able to borrow a big target air rifle, or a .410 shotgun when the occasion warranted. These weapons were useful for dealing with roosting pigeons.

School meanwhile was very different from the classwork of earlier years. Much of my time was taken up in private study with occasional reference to a master. Acting had reduced my prospects of success both because of the time taken in learning parts and rehearsal, and in the distraction provided by favourable newspaper reports encouraging thoughts of a professional stage career. I kept up my studies but had little hope of passing examinations in the summer. My plan to learn German was now in peril, the master who had taught the language for years had now left, replaced by a strange chap whose German was hardly more certain than mine.

However, it was time to give serious thought to my future. I would not be my own master until my twenty first birthday, until then I must pay attention to the views of my parents, more especially since I myself had no knowledge of possible careers and no special inclinations one way or another since outgrowing years previously my early ambition to be an engine driver.

Their reasoning was quite straightforward, I had an aptitude for languages, the only place to earn a decent living as a linguist was in the Foreign Service, entry to which would require a Cambridge first from either Trinity or King's college. I had no idea whether a career in the Foreign Service would appeal to me, nor was I confident of attaining first class honours anywhere, but I was content to let matters develop. Father arranged for me to be interviewed at Cambridge by a King's college tutor one afternoon, and similarly at Trinity college the following morning.

We both set out on an early train to London, then continuing on a less comfortable one across the unfamiliar flat lands to Cambridge, where we left our overnight bags at the University Arms hotel before going to the first interview. I must have presented a sorry sort of figure, father sat in on both meetings and did most of the talking, but eventually I was invited to take the scholarship examination during the Christmas vacation. I looked forward to that only because I would be unaccompanied.

The cricket season returned and I became a regular member of the second eleven, developing a talent for bowling swingers. Second eleven matches were played on Saturday mornings, and the rising dew probably helped me. To my great delight I once took five wickets for ten runs, including on one occasion breaking both middle and off stumps. I presume they had been made from inferior wood, because those stumps were new that season.

The Australian touring side were due to play Gloucestershire at Bristol, a three day game starting on a Saturday, and the Duke of Beaufort had arranged a charity match on the village cricket ground at Badminton for the Sunday. This proved a wonderful opportunity to watch present and past great players in action.

Tom Goddard, proprietor both of the Falcon hotel at Painswick and its garage business, not to be confused with his namesake the famous cricket bowler, had a beautiful turquoise Armstrong Siddeley convertible limousine, and he had made up a party including father and his friends, myself included, to go to the match. We all carried picnic food, and on the back carrier were two crates of beer. Chairs and benches ringed the ground, and cars could be drawn up close enough to have a good view. In a small green marquee to our left sat John Arlott ready to provide a humorous commentary on the game.

The Duke's eleven, under his captain Lord Cobham, were opposed to the Gloucestershire team, and his side included several great Australian players of pre-war years, now accompanying the tourists as reporters, and several of the visitors currently playing at Bristol. Gloucestershire were led by Walter Hammond, ably assisted by Charles Barnett, George Emmett, Jack Crapp and Andy Wilson the wicket keeper. George Lambert, Tom Goddard and Sam Cook would provide the bowling attack. Facing them were Lindsay Hassett, O'Reilly Mailey and Fingleton of the pre-war performers, Don Saggers keeping wicket, B. H. Lyon, the retired Gloucestershire captain, Reg Sinfield, by now coach to Clifton College, with Ring and a couple more Australian bowlers to complete the team. It was a really extraordinary assembly of talent, richly deserving the large crowd which packed the ground.

The lunch interval offered more entertainment as we carefully observed what provision others had made for feeding. A couple of stout farmers lifting a huge wicker hamper out of the boot of their car, with a big cider jar, then tucking white napkins in their collars before setting about a cold chicken were fairly typical of the scene, and meat still being rationed they were also the objects of a certain amount of envy.

The boundaries were a little on the short side, and some lively cricket resulted, assisted after lunch by the announcement that Messrs. Harveys of Bristol had put up a case of sherry for the first batsman to hit a six. We watched an exceptionally high scoring game, entertainment of the very best. Unfortunately certain religious groups pursued the Duke about staging this match, and though it was repeated for some years the fixture was eventually discontinued.

Our summer holiday trip this year was to be to Portrush, in the top right hand corner of Ulster as my atlas showed. What attractions it would offer I did not know, but hoping for some sea fishing we packed our pike rods. A long train journey from Gloucester brought us to the great port of Liverpool, where we boarded the big new Ulster Prince ferry. As we watched load after load of magnificent racing motorcycles were craned into the hold, and the saloons and decks were full of men in riding leathers. We soon realised that this was to be the week-end of the Ulster TT races at the Dundrod circuit near Belfast, our ferry being crowded both with competitors and followers of the event.

Fortunately we had cabins booked for the overnight crossing to Belfast where we boarded a train for the long cross-country journey north. Our hotel was comfortable enough, almost in the centre of what I shall always remember as a very windy little town. The weather must have been more of a problem for the many competitors in the Ulster tennis championships which were being contested at Portrush at that time.

Wind is the principal memory of that fortnight, trailing a fishing line into the harbour with a northerly gale on my back. Unfortunately a gull grabbed my bait before it reached the water, and it was messily dead before I could retrieve the hook. Sadder still, it was a little gull, a type then rather rare. Suddenly our regrets were swamped by the sight of dramatic action. The lifeboat launched into the harbour and charged at full speed out through the entrance taking the heavy seas square on its bow. Looking to seaward we saw the great grey mass of an aircraft carrier, apparently stopped about a couple of miles offshore, barely visible in the stormy murk. The carrier was lying across the wind to make a lee for the approaching lifeboat and had lowered a gangway. We guessed that somebody had been injured too badly to be dealt with in the ship's sick bay, and soon the lifeboat came hurrying back carrying a man tightly bundled in a stretcher comprising canvas and a number of longitudinal slats, to pass him to a waiting ambulance. By the time we glanced to seaward again the carrier had disappeared.

A number of small fishing boats operated out of Portrush at that time, each with a crew of two or three men. They were never in harbour in the morning, but returned each day in mid afternoon. Presumably they must be sailing in the early hours. We asked one of the skippers if he would take us out one night, but in view of the weather he told us to come and check each afternoon as he did not want to take us if the sea was likely to be rough.

At last there came an evening when he told us to be down at the boat at one in the morning. The weather was breezy but dry as we stepped aboard this small vessel, barely thirty feet long, with a little sentry box wheelhouse aft, a foremast wrapped in its sail sloped back and lashed to the wheelhouse roof. The open hold occupying the mid section of the boat contained nets, and would later hold fish as well, the engine filled the after part, while the bow just had room to wedge in a couple of hammocks. On deck a winch was mounted across the stern and another at the bow. There was no rail, and no provision for passengers, we simply had to stand with the right arm through the sail lashings on the mast, grasping the right wrist firmly with the left hand.

By dawn we had motored westward along the coast to a point off the entrance to Lough Foyle. A tall marker flag was floated overboard, and we turned south west paying out a long heavy rope. Then came a turn right and the net was lowered overboard, finally a second right turn and another long rope uncoiled as we returned to the marker flag. At that point one rope was fixed to the stern winch, the other to the bow hauler.

Now we were in full daylight, the winches gradually hauling the net back to the boat. We became aware that we were completely at the mercy of the weather since the angle of boat to wind was now controlled by those two ropes. No longer could we turn head to wind if the need arose. Very soon the wind increased, blowing straight out of the lough, and the effect was extremely dramatic.

High across a wave crest we were looking at hundreds of yards of dripping ropes while straight below where we stood the storm petrels were running along the wave trough. The next moment those ropes were vanishing into a blue wall of water only a few feet from my face, and far higher than the boat, until miraculously our craft suddenly shot up to the crest once more and the sequence was repeated. This was high drama and a quite unforgettable experience, but as time wore on the novelty gave way to boredom and the sort of yawns I associate with seasickness. I managed to fend off the urge, but my brother had taken pills as a precaution, and now he fell asleep. With a good deal of difficulty we took him below and lashed him in a hammock. I returned to my place, arm firmly through sail lashings as the haul continued.

Eventually the net appeared, and lifted aboard revealed some small dogfish rather than the flatfish the skipper had been seeking. The weather was now calmer and having moved on a few miles the tackle was once again laid out and another haul commenced. My brother had woken and resumed his place on deck in the warm morning sun which now helped to revive us from the deep chill caused by standing inactive in the wind for so long.

Hauling brought no drama this time, but the catch was little better, and we headed back toward Portrush, the crew sorting the few fish and stowing the nets. Held by my arm to the rhythmic movement of the mast as we had pitched, rolled or both through the long hours, legs flexing this way and that to compensate for the motion of the boat, I felt I had succeeded rather well in adjusting to the conditions.

Despite our years, I was now approaching eighteen, anxious parents awaited us on the quayside, rather unfortunately I later felt. As we walked along the harbour my brother was in no difficulty, but I who had adjusted so readily to the motion of the boat, or so I thought, was tottering and weaving like a drunken man. In fact I had adjusted rather too well, and now the relentlessly level and firm ground caught me out. By the time I had managed to walk fifty yards I was quite violently sick.

The wind had not finished with me yet. The next day as I walked round a corner in the town during yet another big blow I was lifted bodily and dumped, still standing, in the middle of the cross-roads. Fortunately there were less wild days when buses introduced us to the local attractions of the strange rock formations known as the Giant's Causeway, and the pretty distillery at Bushmills.

Three years after the end of the war rationing remained an ever present restraint to the British, and one of the major attractions of a visit to Ulster lay in the fact that it was possible to visit Eire on a day trip. The Republic had not suffered rationing and reports of feasting on products not seen in England for nine years encouraged a busy trade for the coach operators. Of course we too had to join that hungry stream, and fortunately chose a fine day for the magnificent scenic trip to Bundoran on

Donegal bay. A long drive through varying countryside eventually reached the pretty town of Enniskillen and then skirted the very beautiful Lough Erne with its innumerable islands. To the eye of a keen angler this was close to Paradise.

We found the border at Belleek, famous for its basket-woven chinaware, and soon we were in Bundoran. Here the beach faced the open Atlantic, but nobody on our coach was going to waste time on the beach. It had been a long journey, and now we were going to do some serious eating. We found a table in one of the many cafes and were served a meal the like of which I have never since eaten. A big pot of tea arrived, a dish of warm home-made scones oozing real farm butter, then plates of thick sliced local cured ham and big fried eggs, with lovely moist fruitcake to finish the job. In England rationing would continue for a further six years, that meal remained a beacon of hope never to be forgotten.

Returning home I found that I had failed my Higher Certificate examination, hardly surprisingly in view of all the theatrical work that I had undertaken, but it hurt nonetheless and I worked off my disappointment driving the Atco mower through big lawns which were nearly out of control after our absence in Ireland. A couple of quiet days fishing helped to restore a proper sense of proportion and enabled me to think out a clear plan for the next school year.

My chances of learning sufficient German were quite hopeless, the new teacher had only stayed two terms, and now his lean figure was replaced by a spherical central European with pebble glasses and acute breathing difficulties. His gutturals splattered the pupils and left him constantly wiping his chin.

To pass Higher Certificate it was necessary to score six points. A subsidiary pass was worth one point, main subject level pass scored two, and advanced pass three points. Prudence dictated that one aimed for a minimum of seven points.

Dropping my subsidiary German required that I must now take both English and French to advanced level, being fairly sure that I could pass subsidiary Latin.

The change involved me in studying a large additional number of set books, but I felt confident that I could meet my target. Obviously I did not want to be distracted by other tasks in this last year at school. Boys who had left after their School Certificate year were now visiting in National Service uniforms, those of us who had stayed to take a sixth form course having been granted deferment of call-up to complete our studies. I now obtained a further extension of deferment to take Higher Certificate a second time. What would happen after that was soon resolved.

Following my interviews at Cambridge with my father I was called in December to sit the scholarship examinations there. The university term was over and the colleges were almost empty. I was led up a winding stair to a tiny room with an iron bed, a grate across one corner, a gas ring and half a bucket of coal. The weather was very cold and I was completely demoralised. Breakfast was provided but not much more. The first night I slept in my overcoat, and then found on arrival at the examination hall that it was grossly overheated. Nevertheless I felt I had done reasonably well in the written papers that day.

In the evening I decided to find somewhere warm and went to an Indian restaurant in the town, not realising that I was already unwell. Having spent the night vomiting and shivering I returned to the hot examination hall. Somehow I got through the session, and later quite enjoyed the French oral test. The real problem arose the following morning, when I was booked to take a German oral examination. For some reason word had not passed to Cambridge that I was not now offering German.

The result was pure farce, for although I had a fair understanding of the language in basic terms, I had no intention of attempting to speak it. I knocked on the examiner's study door and was called, in German, to enter. I did so and greeted him in English. I was reminded in very careful German that this was an oral examination and all the conversation had to be conducted in that tongue. I explained my circumstances and that I was unable to speak German, sticking to slowly delivered English. The examiner was very kind, he clearly wanted to be able to enter some sort of score for me, but eventually after about five minutes he accepted my explanations, and I was able to say good-bye, in English.

This was the last test and I quickly collected my bags and made for the station. By now I felt really ill, and went straight to bed when I reached home late that evening. Next day the doctor was summoned and taking one look in my eyelids and between my fingers told me that I had been suffering from jaundice for about a week. He was right, I had a miserable Christmas, full recovery took several weeks, and I was not offered a place at Cambridge. I must now work hard enough to pass Higher Certificate and then await my call-up, aiming for the highest rank I could reach during my service.

I had hoped to enjoy a day pike fishing before the start of the school term, but I was not sufficiently recovered from jaundice. It was not until the 31st of January 1949 that I once again visited Grist's mill with a friend. The weather was chill and gloomy, though the lake was not frozen, and the little boat, half full of water was at least still floating at its moorings. It was soon apparent that this could be a good day. I had cast a live bait from the bank while we baled the boat, and despite the disturbance we made emptying it a five pound pike ran away with my bait almost immediately. I had heard it said that pike feed by moonlight for preference, and we had had a long sequence of cloudy moonless nights. Whether that was the reason for our success I do not know.

We pushed out in the boat to the middle of the little lake and I quickly hooked a big fish, big by the standards of that water at any rate. It weighed ten pounds six ounces, and was thirty six inches long. From a richer feeding water a fish of that length might have weighed half as much again according to the old Mona's scale of pike weights to length. A little later I landed another long thin pike, seven pounds ten ounces, and at thirty four inches long that could have been a twelve pounder. Half an hour later another five pound fish was landed, and then the sport was over, as so often seems to happen without obvious explanation. Once again the big wet hessian sack was dumped in the luggage locker under the stairs as I returned home on the bus, and varying lengths of fish were distributed around father's friends.

I had returned to school to find yet another trap to divert me from my studies. Music was not one of my gifts and my parents' best efforts to have me taught the piano had failed many years earlier. I had sung in the school choir for a number of years, though never as a soloist, I far preferred my quiet country pursuits.

In each school year there emerged a few gifted musicians, and it was on these that each school house now had to rely for the production of choral pieces for performance in the inter house music competition, and subsequent concert. In the previous two years I had not become involved, but now my house had been left without any talented musician at the top, and the lot fell on me. The requirement was performance of one unison song and one part song, and I opted for two simple and familiar tunes which our scratch choir could quickly polish, Schubert's Trout and the Londonderry Air. In the competition we were not disgraced, and at the evening concert I appeared resplendent in father's evening tails, baton in hand, to conduct not only our little choir in front of me, but the accompanying Oxford String Orchestra behind me at one and the same time. It will remain, so far as I am concerned a unique event.

As summer term and the vital examinations approached father decided to return once more to La Baule for our summer holiday, for the first time since 1938. As the language scholar of the family I was expected to telephone the hotel we had visited previously and make the arrangements. When the operators finally made the connection I found myself talking to M. Jacques Boivin, son of the proprietor we had known before the war. The young Jacques had only recently joined the management when we last visited La Baule, but he was immediately able to recall our room numbers from that year, and asked if we would like to have the same ones again. I had to explain that my grandparents were now dead, there would now only be four in the party, and that we could only stay two weeks because of the very tight limit on foreign currency that we could bring. Jacques explained that his parents too had died during the war, though not at the hands of the Germans, he was now in charge and would be visiting London in the autumn to buy furniture. Therefore he would be happy to accept our sterling draft for any expenditure at the hotel if we were short of francs. I wondered what we would find, visiting once again this place I had so loved as a little boy, since when it had experienced war, something of which I had hardly any knowledge.

It was time for the Higher Certificate examinations, and this year I felt less apprehensive of the outcome. The various papers were taken at sufficient intervals to enable revision, without which I could not have survived the test because of the very large number of books I had studied in that final year. The weather was merciful, not quite so hot as in earlier years when the perspiration ran down my pen and threatened to drip on my paper. After each session I was able to feel a great burden lifted, as another pile of books could be set aside, never to be read again. When it was all over we stayed on until the end of term to discharge our various prefectorial duties, and then finally we left.

And so at last I completed ten years at the school which had welcomed a terribly shy little stranger in the autumn of 1939. In little more than another two years I would be of age, and my own master, meanwhile still lacking any vision of a future career, I would see how much National Service could broaden my horizons and my experience. I felt sure that by the time I was discharged I would have a clear idea of the course I wanted to follow.

My brother returned from the Conway, and the family set out for France. Living in Gloucestershire this was no longer a matter of taking an express from Waterloo to Southampton, rather we would travel from Cheltenham on a quiet little track that meandered through the countryside and across Salisbury Plain to that same port. All the railways I knew seemed to fan out from the great cities, this little branch line puzzled me. I wondered whether it had been built to carry supplies, munitions and men in the first world war.

War was going to be in the forefront of our minds in the next few weeks as we saw the dreadful devastation still so evident even after four years of re-building. Southampton, terribly damaged gave us some inkling of what we would find in Brittany. But first we had the sea crossing in a magnificent new ferry, one of the first I was told, to be fitted with a gyro stabiliser. We went aboard, found our cabins and had a meal as she sailed into the calm summer evening.

It was much later, in the early hours, when the wind increased somewhat and we entered the awkward seas of the

Jersey Race that the stabiliser was switched on, and I found the effect most uncomfortable. The ship would start a roll, but then suddenly stop, hold for a few moments before starting the opposite roll and then abruptly stop that motion again. An ordinary rhythmic movement I could happily accept, that strangely ruptured roll I found most uncomfortable.

Consequently I was on deck in good time for our early morning arrival at St. Malo. I had been too young to remember the place on my previous visit, but I needed no comparisons to underline for me the terrible devastation the war had brought. Buckled and rusting sea defences, shattered concrete emplacements, areas bombed flat extended in all directions both in the port and along the coast. I wondered what sort of holiday this poor ruined land could offer us. At least it would be a history lesson that had not been taught in my school years.

Once again our route varied from the railway we had followed before the war, this time a long distance high speed bus would take us to our destination. It warned of its approach with a sustained blast from twin electric trumpets on the roof, quite sufficient to make a passenger's hair stand on end. We saw less of the countryside than when travelling by train because hedges frequently blocked the view, and most of the villages we passed seemed unprotected by speed limits so far as our bus was concerned.

Arriving at our hotel amid the long remembered pine woods with their resinous perfume little seemed to have changed. The war had left few scars on La Baule, although some of the major hotels were only now re-opening after being requisitioned for other purposes by the Germans. That magnificent stretch of sand beach still gleamed in the bright August sun, and I could see no trace of any sea defences there. Perhaps the fact that the water is very shallow for a long way offshore had made it appear a very unlikely front on which to mount an attack.

Our interests now were different, long past sandcastle building we hired flotteurs. These comprised a pair of metal tubes with conical end caps, fastened about a yard apart by a slatted wooden seat, and by a separate footrest. A double paddle was provided and we set off rather kayak fashion to explore the length of the beach. It made a change from walking and dodging other people, while giving an excellent view of what was going on. It was apparent that plenty of visitors were spending their holidays at what had been noted before the war as a favourite resort of Parisians.

The gymnastic clubs were still there with their great climbing frames and creches where parents could discard their children, and we noticed that among the younger adults volleyball was becoming popular. Watching the crashing dives the players so often had to make I could well appreciate that the game was best played on soft sand. Of course we had to see what was being landed by the local fishermen, and took the bus to Le Croisic as we had done eleven years earlier. A great variety from tuna to sardines, crawfish to crevettes were being landed, Le Croisic obviously still had its trade.

A large area nearby was devoted to the production of sea salt. An extensive network of little square ponds bounded by narrow trackways covered the low lying land and each spring tide the sea refilled these shallow ponds. Evaporation left a thick salty scum which was collected and piled to dry where paths crossed. Sunshine dried out the mass and the result was natural sea salt.

I felt that prosperity would soon return to La Baule, already the polo club was busy, and occasionally a passenger aircraft would land at the aerodrome at La Baule Escoublac. A few miles down the coast however a lot of rebuilding remained to be done. St. Nazaire had been a very important naval base and dry dock during the war and it had been comprehensively and repeatedly bombed. On the 28th March 1942 a brilliant commando raid had put the dry dock out of action, but the immensely thick concrete roofs over the submarine pens were still in place when we visited the town and such of the naval base area as was not restricted. Between La Baule and St. Nazaire the contrast was really shocking.

Our fortnight was soon over, and that high speed bus hurried us back to St. Malo and the overnight ferry to Southampton. It was a calm crossing, but in the morning we found the approach to the port totally obscured by very thick shallow fog. We could look up and see the blue sky, but all around our visibility was almost nil. As our berthing time approached more and more passengers came on deck to the open observation area immediately below the navigation bridge. Unable to see, passengers and crew were all silent, listening intently, the ferry hardly moving.

As a trainee mariner my brother had a professional interest in the proceedings and we had found our place immediately below the man on the navigating bridge who seemed to be in charge of our docking. He picked up his microphone, and his measured delivery was amplified to an enormous noise by the loud-hailer amplifier "Antonia, Antonia can you hear me?" The response was immediate, a thunderous foghorn blast apparently a few degrees off our port bow, and only a matter of feet away from our ship.

*Antonia* was the ferry from the Channel Islands, already tied up on her berth immediately ahead of ours. We had in fact managed to come within a few yards of our destination without even being able to see the quay. We were soon safely moored, but I learned something about fog at sea which came frequently to mind in later years.

Back home once more up that lovely little country railway line, I had passed Higher Certificate and must now wait for my

National Service call-up. The system provided that one could express a preference for a particular service or regiment, but I had already decided that the army would best make use of my cadet experience. I had no connections with the county regiment, my ambitions extended no further than obtaining my driving licence, not least because father's ever widening interests so clearly demonstrated that his inability to drive was a serious drag on his efficiency. Not that I had any intention of becoming his chauffeur, but the need to be able to drive was particularly obvious to me. I had asked to join the Royal Army Service Corps, whose duties roughly comprised providing transport and supplies to the army. The further extent of their involvement I would discover later.

I heard nothing until mid October, but there were plenty of interests to occupy me. Old enough now to be allowed in the local pubs I soon heard the various little bits of local news that did not always reach the papers for one reason or another. This was a time when military aircraft were rather less in evidence, but civil aviation seemed to be expanding rapidly. Much of the news concerned developments in the United States or in the home counties, but just thirty miles to the south of my home they were building a giant airliner, the Brabazon.

At Filton, north of Bristol an especially long runway had been built because provision needed to be in place for the first flight of this monster craft to be a straight line hop, takeoff and landing on the same runway without turning. Rumour had it that the test pilot, who lived at Minchinhampton, not far away, hoped to do better than that; also that the maiden flight would take place the following day, Sunday 4th September.

My brother and I felt that this was certainly not an event to be missed, but our home was unsighted from Filton by the wold edge at North Nibley. This would be a bicycle job, but rather than go all the way to Bristol we would cycle down into the Severn vale flat lands keeping a good eye open to southwards.

We were down there in good time, though expecting the flight not to commence until after gentlemanly Sunday breakfast. It must have been about mid-day, as I cycled westward in the direction of the river somewhere near Moreton Valence that I spotted this huge aircraft in the sky towards Bristol. I was in front of my brother at that point, and pointed at the plane, gave a signal that I was slowing down, and stopped.

My brother's cycle, with drop handlebars unlike my upright model, had him riding in a head-down position. He saw no signal and rode straight into my back wheel, my mudguard slashing my tyre.

Fortunately neither of us was seriously hurt, and my brother's cycle could still be ridden. As for mine, it would have to be wheeled along on the front wheel only, or carried if the rear wheel rim was to escape damage. Brother set off for home, and would send a taxi down my agreed route when he arrived. Fortunately the weather was fine, though not too hot, but I had brought my cycle back about six miles before the car arrived. Despite a nasty anti-climax we had indeed seen the Brabazon on its first flight, and would not forget the circumstances of that day.

We had been helping with the harvest, gathering the stooked sheaves onto carts and taking them to the barn. The two little carthorses, Punch and Tommer still found employment at that time when there was more work than the old utility Fordson tractor with its spiked iron wheels could handle. I had learned how to collect the horses and back them into the cart shafts before fastening their tackle and pushing a small branch of elder under the browband to ward off flies. It was a pleasant enough occupation leading the cart out, helping to load it, and then bringing it back under the shade of the elms to the barn for stacking.

My brother returned to his training ship, and I found work in the garden, where the row of lime trees on the eastward boundary needed lopping. I was still living at home free of charge of course, and felt obliged to try in some way to earn my keep. Then came the day when the contract threshing machine arrived at the farm, and this year I was really going to do a proper job, rather than shooting emerging rats. Now I would be one of those on that high platform cutting the twine from the sheaves and dropping the corn into the thresher drum.

Having watched so many times I felt quite confident, but in the event I had a dreadful shock. As I slit open one sheaf a fieldmouse dropped out onto the platform, and dashed straight up inside the leg of my corduroy trousers. Flinging my knife aside, and grabbing the trouser leg tightly at the knee I performed a back somersault off the platform and onto a pile of straw below. Without thinking I pushed my free hand up the trouser leg to grab the animal, at which point it grabbed me. Pulling out my painful hand I found the little creature had bitten the end of my forefinger, from which it now dangled, its long sharp teeth having met through my flesh. I wondered why it had taken me so many years to realise why farm workers wore gaiters or tied their trousers at the knee. One more lesson had been learned the hard way, by experience.

My call-up papers arrived, including a one way rail travel warrant, third class, to Aldershot where I was to report on 3rd November. My last few weeks as a civilian were devoted to some seasonable activities. As the beech leaves changed to brown, the water lilies died down and the time for pike fishing had returned. I had no spare cash for trout baits, but using my bicycle I could ride to the mill, setting a float tackle to fish for livebait, while trying to tempt the pike with a spinner. I had not often used a spinner there before, but it proved quite a successful method of fishing.

    Then lock the cycle in the garage, put rods and tackle carefully away and walk up to the Falcon for a pint of bitter. To-morrow I will have to catch that train and grow up.

# CHAPTER 11

To reach Aldershot by train it was necessary to change at Reading, but the early express to Paddington did not stop there. Fewer people waited for the later stopping train but I found myself looking around to see whether any other passengers might be in my call-up group. I could see none, and again when changing trains onto the Southern rail line at Reading I could not be sure how many other passengers were new recruits. At Aldershot all was quickly revealed, and we were shepherded onto covered lorries fitted with a row of seats down each side and another bench down the middle. Soon we were at our new home, Oudenarde barracks, built many years previously in long low blocks comprising pairs of single storey dormitories, each pair linked by a small washroom and lavatory block, and a room where the corporal in charge lived.

A dormitory block accommodated a line of beds down each side, each with its locker. In the middle of the room a black polished coke stove stood, its flue extending upwards through the roof. Having left our baggage on a bed we were led off to the stores, and made our acquaintance for the first of many times with the extraordinarily ugly army verb, to be issued with. Two pairs of boots, brown gym shoes, socks wool, drawers wool, vests wool, gloves wool, Jersey wool, shirts, tie, battledress trousers and blouse, web belt, anklets, greatcoat and beret, plus a kitbag that might be big enough to contain part of the pile.

The corporal in charge of my billet, always known to us as Monty, showed us how to label and store all this kit, which also included a set of boot polishing brushes on which we used metal dies to impress the last four digits of our army number in case at any time they might be borrowed. Those brushes would over time do a lot of work. The many who had never had to polish brass buttons and buckles before were introduced to the button stick, a slotted strip of brass, which when slipped round the button to be polished protected the fabric beneath from soiling. Then too it was necessary to be introduced to one other small item, a little cotton pouch called a housewife, but pronounced hussiff, which contained needles and thread for minor clothing repairs. That needed to be stowed where it could easily be found, but not where it might be carelessly grasped and its needles run into a hand.

Then we were shown how bedding must be arranged, made up meant that after washing, shaving and dressing all sheets and blankets were to be neatly folded and piled at the head of the bed, blankets and sheets in alternate order and all showing the same width across the front of the pile, the whole topped out with the pillow. At the end of the working day the bed could be made down, the expression used to describe its form when ready to receive its tired occupant.

I had been among the earlier arrivals, and through the rest of the day more lorries brought their loads to the barracks, until at last an intake of six hundred and sixty had arrived. We must all have seemed rather bewildered, but the army had been handling this sort of day for a long time, and it was soon obvious that the system worked. My principal impression concerned accent. Suddenly I was surrounded by young men from all over the country, many of whom I found almost incomprehensible. My ear, comfortably attuned to soft Gloucestershire tones suddenly had to translate voices from Birmingham, Glasgow, Cornwall, Liverpool and Yorkshire.

We were of course a very mixed bunch, some with little educational qualification, and having deferred my call-up I was nearly a year older than most. The army now had to sort us out in accordance with our inclinations and abilities and post us to the units where we would get the right training.

The sorting out process naturally took a good deal of time, but in the course of a fortnight we were all interviewed and categorised whether by trade, training or inclination.

Meanwhile we had to learn to fall in three ranks and to march, then perform simple movements such as wheeling and turning. Moving at speed with high armswings, early morning drill parade quickly warmed us on those very cold November days. Back in our billet corporal Monty showed us how to lay out our kit for inspection, and explained what needed blanco and what Duraglit. Our individual bed spaces must be kept clean and tidy, and we would take turns fuelling the stove, sweeping the main floor, and on inspection mornings polishing both floor and stove.

For the first week we were confined to barracks, but the food was sufficient, we had our own little NAAFI which sold blanco, polish, sweets and cigarettes, which were all that we were likely to buy until our first pay day. Medical examinations had left us rather unwell, since they included vaccination and a number of injections, of which the worst was the TAB. Immediately after that jab we were taken onto the parade ground and marched rapidly round with shoulder high armswings, the theory being that to quickly circulate the injected fluid would lessen adverse symptoms later. In fact a very painful arm and a temperature running high for two days was not uncommon.

After that first pay parade, when we stepped forward, signed the book, took our little handful of notes and coins, stepped back, saluted, turned and marched out, those of us not on fatigue or guard duty could go into Aldershot. We must at all times wear uniform, be properly dressed, and carry our service book for identification purposes.

We made an important discovery, in the middle of Aldershot was a new NAAFI club, with snooker tables, restaurant and reading room, all very comfortably furnished and warm. Despite the distance from our barracks its attractions well justified our effort in walking there. This club was something to remember whatever unit we might subsequently be sent to.

Now at last the sorting out was complete, and sixteen of us were sent to Blackdown camp to take an OR/1 course. Others went to a variety of destinations, some far from Aldershot, to train as drivers, mechanics, cooks and so forth, and the staff at Oudenarde were ready to receive their next batch of raw material.

I had thought our old barracks cold, but Blackdown was far colder. A hutted camp, it backed onto the wooded edge of an east facing scarp above the famous Bisley rifle ranges, and the winter wind swept ruthlessly through it.

Socially however it was really delightful. In that great jumble of humanity at Oudenarde it had been difficult to find anybody with whom one shared an interest, and it had been just as well that I was used to my own company. Now every one of our group were interesting educated men, most from a public school background, all lively and very keen. With the exception of a couple who decided later to train for a clerical NCO role, we were all ready to work as hard as necessary to be commissioned.

We had just eight weeks in which to sharpen our performance before the searching process of the War Office Selection Board, and we had all the enthusiasm needed. Our billet was at the farthest edge of the camp, the NAAFI a draughty walk away by the main entrance, and often cash was short, with the result that evenings became busy with boot polishing and animated conversation.

We were now equipped with rifles, bayonets, helmets and packs, the scope for cleaning and polishing was endless. To properly clean a rifle was a lengthy and precise business, especially if you had fallen somewhere on the assault course at the back of the camp, where we now regularly exercised. We had all selected one pair of boots for ordinary wear and the other for drill. Gradually the drill boots were acquiring an almost glazed appearance as more and more spit and polish built up. Morning drill parades were really stimulating. All of us had freshly pressed battledress blouses, our trouser creases proclaimed that they had spent the night under the mattress, our badges and belt brasses shone.

Our ambition was to go to Mons officer cadet school, renowned for the standards of its drill, where RSM Brittain had charge of the square. That aim quickened and tidied our marching and rifle drill day by day, encouraged by excellent NCOs. There is a stage at which, far from being drudgery, drill with a tightly integrated high performance team becomes exhilarating, further enhancing the performance.

After four weeks they gave us return travel warrants and sent us home for Christmas, to rejoin our unit on Boxing Day. That nine days was a welcome break, but less than a month ahead lay the great selection board hurdle, that was where my real interest lay.

We had been introduced to rifle shooting, most of us having had school or club smallbore experience already had little difficulty using the short Lee-Enfield .303. The Bren machine gun was a delightful weapon, and that too we now had a chance to fire on the ranges. The physical training instructors were pushing us hard over the assault course now, but we were only too keen to improve our strength and speed. We had struck up a particularly happy relationship with them because their gym, just behind our billet, was equipped for basketball. The PTIs were all very tall, as were a number of our course, including myself. We had people who had played the game before, and soon we were all going to the gym as soon as our day ended to dash around with a basketball.

Still the drill boots shone more brightly, the uniform creases sharpened, and then at last, a few weeks into 1950, came the summons to attend the selection board at Barton Stacey. We had practised hard for this, having been told of some of the ingredients of the process but the actual event, our only chance to continue to a commission, was a very major occasion.

Over the two days we were interviewed, dined in groups with our examiners, discussed hypothetical problems and dealt with the sort of practical puzzle that places six men, a pole, a forty gallon drum and a length of rope on one side of a chasm, the object being to get all the men and equipment to the other side. Then too we each had to deliver a five minute lecturette on a subject of our own choice. I instructed my audience on stalking and killing a rabbit with a catapult. This was something I knew nobody else on my course had done, and I felt afterwards that it had gone down very well, though one judge had just that suggestion of a smile which might indicate that he thought my tale a rather clever fiction.

We returned to Blackdown, all but two of us had passed and I was one of the lucky ones. We now had a week on leave before our move to Mons. We would spend six weeks at the officer cadet school doing regimental training, that is to say the sort of thing required of every soldier whatever his speciality, followed by ten weeks at Buller barracks, the RASC headquarters, where we would train in the technical aspects of the work of the corps.

Hair was worn very short in the army, and at Mons, we had been warned, it was worn even shorter. To save time I visited the village barber before returning from leave for an extra short back and sides. I wasted my money because as soon as we arrived at the officer cadet school we were sent to the camp barber, and thereafter had our hair cut twice a week.

Now we were accommodated in billets similar to the old brick blocks at Oudenarde, but kit layout for inspection had been exquisitely refined. The basis was the so-called Mons bed. Blankets and sheets were laid on the mattress, folded back to show alternate bands of blanket and sheet, all of equal width, down the length of the bed. Each line of beds was then precisely aligned with the aid of a length of string so that viewed from the door the stripes of blankets and sheets were continuous along the length of the room. When total accuracy had been accomplished each bed was then tucked in and ironed, before adding such equipment as was to be displayed. Last man out retreated backwards on hands and knees on an old blanket, with which he carefully rubbed out the last footprints leaving an unbroken shine on the floor.

We had now been joined by groups of people from various other corps, who having passed through a similar selection process to ourselves would now share the joys of six weeks at Mons before continuing with technical training in their own units. Together we were now close to company strength, and not surprisingly it took a little while to sharpen up the drill of this more numerous parade. All the company sergeant majors were guardsmen, Tall, lean and ramrod straight, each using his pace stick to constantly check the length of our stride.

Once knocked into shape we found ourselves marching onto the square to join all the other companies of the school, plus the two units that stayed at Mons for their ten weeks corps training, stretched out several units abreast and several deep across the square, now under the command of regimental sergeant major Brittain. Several inches taller than the CSMs and twice their girth, he was a formidable figure indeed. From his position at centre front he made his voice carry to the uttermost corners of the parade, so that every man in every unit followed his command simultaneously. That was the objective, and to ensure that it was achieved each company sergeant major stood facing his unit ready to correct any mistake or vocally encourage any idler. Often it was the RSM himself who spotted the odd one out "Sergeant Major Scott, man third from the right, second rank, pull on his butt." There in our block in the distant rear of the whole parade a sloped rifle was immediately brought a little nearer the vertical.

Those early parades helped to warm us in the cold February mornings, though we had of course already breakfasted. Nobody skipped breakfast, fainting on parade was not a frequent occurrence, but to miss breakfast and then faint on parade was an offence resulting in a charge.

After our work on the square we moved to hot little lecture rooms where various subjects were explored, I remember in particular the dapper little major from the Bedfordshire and Hertfordshire regiment "Not the beds and hearts" who instructed us in military law. Most of his illustrations involved Second Lieutenant N. O. Hope and Private Parts. We dealt with a wide range of matters, even including treason felony, an offence we were told against the King's eldest daughter, but we would rarely need to stray beyond the good old 'conduct prejudicial to good order and military discipline'. The tiered lecture hall was hot and stuffy, many of us had a struggle to remain awake.

Our status had changed, and we had been too busy to notice. White georgette patches, each topped with a small brass button had been stitched to the lapels of our battledress blouses. The white part must be immaculately blancoed, the button highly polished for these patches identified us as officer cadets. All the non-commissioned instructors now addressed us as Sir, which oddly enough could become a very humbling mode of address.

Lectures on infantry tactics, fire and movement and the

like, which those of us with cadet force experience already understood, were put into practice in exercises on the training areas around Aldershot. Years of stalking rabbits left me in no difficulty when using cover, wind and dead ground in an approach. Now however things were made more difficult. We would carry full equipment, including trenching tools, and the programme was extended to twenty four hours. Tired after half a day of the exercise we found ourselves in the gathering darkness of a late February evening being told that we had five minutes to get underground.

Working in pairs in full kit we shovelled frantically at the sand and flints of the Long Valley, and promptly after five minutes the Thunderflash practice grenades and blank rifle fire started. We eventually excavated a two man weapon slit, where a few hours later we wrapped our greatcoats in our groundsheet cloaks and snatched a bit of sleep. Before dawn we were on the move again along a stretch of the Basingstoke canal, walking in line ahead through swirling fog. We were to mount an attack on an unseen silent enemy through rough birch scrub, and my fieldcraft experience was not sufficient to ensure a safe approach. Our load of kit offered so many straps ready to snag on a low branch, and if my mess tins did not rattle at a critical moment somebody else's would. It was a trying business, but we reached our objective in the end.

Dawn gave way to unseasonable sunshine and we sweated miserably as we reached the climax of the outing, a charge up a long steep sand slope, led by a particularly fit instructor, a slim Irish captain who took two Bren guns, and with one on each shoulder ran all the way to the top. The umpires kept a close eye on us there, one or two had to be given a bit of help.

On the ranges we had plenty of rifle practice, and all reached the standard expected of us. Physical training was not a problem, though I disliked the boxing session. Some of our number had boxed at school, I had not. We were required to fight three three-minute rounds under strict amateur rules, the instructors matching opponents without weighing. I really hated the idea. I did not mind learning to shoot people, but the idea of somebody thumping my skinny frame, even with a big sparring glove I found quite disgusting. At six foot two inches and ten stone I was matched against a slightly tubby ex public school man with previous experience of the sport. Gritting my teeth I set about my task to such effect that I won on points. That had not been my intention. In the next contest I made sure that I was beaten, sparing myself further exposure in later eliminators.

Drilling on the square had become ever more complex and precise, slow and quick march past in line were now a part of the routine, we were rehearsing for the passing-out parade of one of the senior units. Our own departure to technical training was only a week or two away when we heard a wonderful piece of news. The army football final, to be held at the stadium just down the road from our lines would be attended by the King, and our little company was to provide a route lining guard of honour at the entrance to the stadium. As we approached the end of that era of intensive spit and polish it was exhilarating to think that we would now have an opportunity to show off in public.

The RSM himself marched us down to the stadium entrance to measure off where we would stand. One line of men extended diagonally on each side of the entrance to the edge of the road, others in each direction along the pavement edge, with a corresponding single line on the opposite side of the road. I found myself just to the left of the entrance, and by the time we had pushed out to arms length apart I was a little alarmed to find that I had both feet on a flimsy looking manhole cover. Given the force with which my heel hit the ground when performing the salute I was worried that it might signal my instant disappearance into the Aldershot sewers.

On the great day we took our positions in good time, a number of very senior officers assembled to greet the monarch, RSM Brittain stood just to my right. We had sloped arms, and now as the royal car slowed and stopped came the operative command.

"Mons Officer Cadet School, royal salute, present arms". How he could time his delivery so precisely I do not know, but the fact remains that the final word was pronounced at the very instant when the King's foot touched the red carpet. My heel crashed down with some dozens of others, the manhole cover held, and as the hair-raising drumroll led the band into the national anthem I was struck by the fact that this rather small man appeared to be wearing make-up.

We marched back to our quarters, and a few days later moved on down the road towards Aldershot, to our new home at Buller barracks where we would spend the next ten weeks. It was nearly Easter, and the big trees which were a characteristic of that place were beginning to show green, it was nice to feel that the next phase of training would take place in lengthening and warmer days.

Our original group from Blackdown had been somewhat augmented by some men who had now transferred to the RASC, but we were no more than a platoon strength group. In charge on the square was the very erect but considerably rotund figure of company sergeant major Mortimore. Any slight tendency to relax after the rigours of Mons was quickly corrected, and he allowed himself a rather more relaxed form of speech than the Mons staff, though still remembering to address us correctly. On the occasion when one of our number turned the wrong way on morning parade I remember his booming, drawn out comment "you dizzy bugger, Sir".

The Royal Army Service Corps dealt with matters of

supplies and transport, our training would concentrate on the latter, while we would be given an introduction to the other duties of the corps. Much of our time was spent in overalls learning the intricacies of the internal combustion engine, After all, we were expected to emerge from here each to take charge of a transport platoon. We would of course have workshops and mechanics to help, but at least we must know how to conduct a vehicle inspection and recognise common defects.

Now too we were being taught to drive. Our instructors each took four of us in a three ton Bedford OY canvas topped lorry to a quiet stretch of road south of the town. Each of us in turn then drove this cumbersome machine around a circuit of roads before stopping to change drivers, whereupon we rejoined the conversation behind the cab. In fine weather it was quite a pleasant way to spend our time, and after some weeks we graduated to the bigger Bedford QL, which we could drive on the training areas. In both vehicles the gearbox had no synchro-mesh, this was learning to drive the original way. Unfortunately none of us reached the level which would have given us our Certificate of Competence to Drive, but we were well on our way to that qualification.

Our contact with other aspects of the work of the corps was limited to one day. A morning spent visiting the abattoir introduced us to slaughtering and butchery, in the afternoon we went to the last remaining horse transport company. Here the officer commanding caught our attention by asking the question "What is the first thing you do if told to back-rake an animal?" The answer was that the right forearm must be shaved and liberally coated with soft soap. The task was manual evacuation of a constipated horse.

At last the reality was dawning, we were all going to be commissioned. Our kit allowances arrived and we set off to London to be measured for our service dress. In addition we needed cap, Sam Browne belt, cane, brown gloves, brown boots, brown shoes, brown trilby and a pale riding mackintosh. Some of these could wait, but the boots and shoes we must take now, in order to have them sufficiently polished by the time we were ready to wear them.

Smartly printed official invitations were produced announcing the date of our passing-out parade in the first week of June, for us to send to parents and relatives. We were invited to express preferences for the area in which we would like to serve, including Germany, Far East, Middle East, Bermuda and Cyprus, the last two of which had only a small RASC element. A friend and I both nominated Cyprus, with little hope of success.

The weeks had sped past, service dresses had now been fitted and collected with the remainder of our officer necessities. To-morrow was the great day, and our evening was taken up cutting georgette patches carefully away from battledress blouses, then stitching a second lieutenant's pip on each shoulder. Next morning we joined a big parade formed from all that group with whom we had first enlisted, who each in their own field had now completed training. The salute was taken on the Polo Ground, the only occasion when I paraded on grass. As our eyes switched right, there beside the inspecting general's rostrum were the proud parents, mine included. A few minutes later, the march-past over, we were able to chat briefly.

They caught the train home, but I went back with my fellow second lieutenants to barracks to finish handing in webbing equipment to stores, to pack ready for departure on leave the next day, and to enjoy a considerable party. The following morning we parted, fully expecting to meet again in the course of our service.

I carefully stowed my two brand new suitcases on the

luggage rack and sat down in the little stopping train that was going to quietly take me through the pretty Berkshire countryside to Reading where I would join the rush and bustle of the main line. I was the only passenger in that compartment, and as I wondered whether I would indeed be posted to Cyprus, and how long my embarkation leave would be, I realised that here, just for a moment was an opportunity for reflection.

How on earth had that little withdrawn unsociable lad who was taken to Stroud in 1939 emerged nearly eleven years later to gain a commission in the army? There was no doubt, whatever post I chose to apply for after my discharge, I would at least be sure of an interview. Here was Reading, I carried my cases across to the busy Great Western station. I could face the future with some confidence.